🟢	Nature's Lessons: A Way of Teaching	2
🟢	Ideas Across the Curriculum: A Whole-Child Approach to Skill Development	6
🟡	Language/Literacy	8
🟢	Science	28
🟣	Social/Emotional	50
🔵	Mathematics	76
🔴	Body Competence	88
🔵	Creative Arts	116
🟤	Visual/Spatial	132
🟢	Final Thoughts	142
🟢	References	143
🟢	Acknowledgements	144

Growing With Nature. Copyright © 2011
by Dimensions Educational Research Foundation. All rights reserved.
For information on how to reproduce portions of this book write:
Permissions: Dimensions Foundation, 1010 Lincoln Mall, Suite 103, Lincoln, NE 68508
ISBN: 978-0-9839465-0-2

Nature's Lessons: A Way of Teaching

**By Nancy Rosenow, Executive Director
Dimensions Educational Research Foundation**

I'll never forget the moment when a five-year-old named Ella taught me a profound lesson about life, and about teaching. I was taking some funders on a quick tour through a nature-filled outdoor classroom when Ella approached us quietly and asked if we'd like to see something special. She pointed to a tree where a delicate light blue eggshell was dangling from a branch. "The baby bird just hatched," she told us in a hushed voice, her dark eyes shining. "Grownups are always in such a hurry. I was afraid you were going to miss this treasure of nature."

What a wake-up call. "Ella," I wanted to say, "*You* are a treasure of nature." And now, looking back, I'm sorry I didn't say it. Our hurried-up lifestyles can all too often cause us to miss much more than just the natural wonders of our world. How often are we grownups in such a hurry for children to master the alphabet, pass the next test or prepare for the next grade that we miss the treasure of who each child is as a unique individual? Are we giving ourselves, and our children, a chance to take a deep breath and enjoy our natural world, enjoy childhood, and enjoy each other? I believe that teaching with nature can be an antidote to our sometimes frantic approach to life in general.

It's no doubt that our children are growing up in a fast-paced world. Technology is a great connector, but it can also demand that we be instantly available to each other, no matter what. And, while it is wonderful to be able to turn on the television and "see" each other all over the world in real time, this often means our children are bombarded with horrific images of war or natural disasters right in their own homes. Where is the "safe haven" for our children these days?

One answer is that nature-filled outdoor classrooms can provide that safe haven. There, away from televisions, video games, smart phones and computers for a brief time each day, the world can slow down and everyone can breathe easier. Children can be children, adults can smile more, and discoveries can unfold slowly, with no expectation of "finding the one right answer."

What doesn't have to slow down, however, is learning.

For over a decade, our Dimensions Foundation teachers and researchers have been documenting the rich learning that happens when children and adults have the time and space to explore nature together. And, as adults all over the nation have built and begun to use what we call "Nature Explore Classrooms," they too are documenting amazing results. Throughout this book you will hear from educators, parents and administrators who believe in teaching with nature. As these wonderful people share their stories, we hope you will discover a few common themes throughout:

- The richest kind of learning happens holistically.

- Children need the time and space to find out and express who they uniquely are.

- Intentionally designed outdoor classrooms can support children in this personally meaningful, whole-child learning. (The space becomes the third teacher.)

- Educators who support learning with nature help make amazing things happen.

- Families who enjoy meaningful experiences in the natural world give children an invaluable gift.

- Volunteers and community members play an important role in helping create effective nature-filled spaces.

- "Magic moments" in nature-filled spaces can enrich a child's life forever.

Our stories come from interviews and some directly from our research. They mostly represent three age-groups: infants and toddlers; preschoolers; and elementary students.

That's because we've done most of our work with those ages over the past decade. Recently we've begun working with middle schools and high schools as parents and others ask, "Why can't this type of learning continue?" As more experiences with these older students are documented, you'll see more of our resources being developed for that age group.

Before you dive into the book, Ella would probably want me to urge you to be sure you take your time and savor the stories so you don't miss the "treasure" in each one. Following some of the stories, we have added a paragraph called "insights" that highlights the importance of the teaching and learning taking place. We invite you to discover insights of your own in each story. You are also invited to visit our Web site, natureexplore.org to view video clips from educators around the country that provide great insights into the value of teaching with nature.

As you discover other people's experiences, perhaps you will think about the children in your own life. Whether you are a teacher, a parent or grandparent, an administrator or a public official, we hope you will gain ideas and inspiration for ways you too can "teach with nature"…or make it possible where you live. And, when you do, it would be wonderful if you would share your own stories. You can send them to us at info@natureexplore.org.

Really, spaces filled with "nature's treasures" simply give us the venue we can use to show our children that our world (despite its "bad news") is still a good place. We all want our children to grow up knowing the world as a place full of wonder, a place worth learning about, a place worth caring for and protecting.

Consider the words of Rachel Carson's on the following page. They were written decades ago in her book, *Sense of Wonder*, and are perhaps more true today than ever before.

"If a child is to keep alive his inborn sense of wonder, he needs the companionship of at least one adult who can share it, rediscovering with him the joy, excitement, and mystery of the world we live in." (Carson, 1965)

We can each be that adult.

Ideas Across The Curriculum

A Whole-Child Approach to Skill Development

By Christine Kiewra and Tina Reeble
Dimensions Educational Research Foundation

We educators love to divide children's learning into "subject areas" or "domains." Doing so is helpful in many ways. By focusing on discrete topics – like language and literacy or science or math – we can assess whether children are developing the many skills and understandings they will need in order to become adults fully equipped to participate in life. But if we're not careful, we can fool ourselves into thinking that learning takes place in segments. In reality, it is crucial for educators and parents to recognize that children learn and develop best when they gain skills holistically. Children are able to develop skills and understandings in many areas at the same time as they engage in personally meaningful explorations of the world around them. This is why learning with nature is such a powerful motivator for holistic development. Dimensions Foundation researchers discussed this concept in a paper written about one of their case studies:

"The first key theme that emerged in our analysis of teachers' Nature Notes suggests that when children were engaged in authentic play in the Nature Explore Classroom they were developing important skills – skills that are foundational for early learning and will be important in helping children successfully navigate in the world…However, one of the most significant findings of this research is that when children were engaged in authentic play in the Nature Explore Classroom, they were developing skills in a variety of domains simultaneously. This is what we refer to as whole-child learning." (Miller, Tichota, White, p. 52)

We also know that learning is powerfully supported by having shared experiences with others. Our Dimensions Foundation research shows that because experiences in Nature Explore Classrooms are so fully engaging, children are inspired to think deeply about their explorations and discuss them with teachers, caregivers, and peers. Truly deep learning happens when children are highly motivated to gain information and then communicate their understandings back to others.

Throughout this book you'll find stories about children's learning with nature that are divided by skill areas (language and literacy skills, science skills, etc.). The important thing to remember about these groupings is that they are artificial and helpful mostly to adults. They don't reflect the holistic way that children really learn.

So, with that caveat, we hope you enjoy these stories that have come to us from people all over the country who are passionate about how connections with the natural world help children grow. You will notice each section is filled with stories from all three age-groups (infants and toddlers, preschoolers and elementary school students). While most of the stories throughout the book come from early childhood programs or elementary schools, we've also tried to include stories about learning that happened in public settings or with families.

Perhaps the most important aspect of the stories you're about to read is in the excitement children demonstrate about learning. Not once is anyone focused on a test a child is about to take. While there is a place for standardized testing in children's lives, we believe those tests are simply one way to document children's learning. (There are many other equally as valuable ways to document learning.) Being able to score well on a test is ultimately not the end goal of our educational system. Inspiring children to see the excitement and purpose of true learning so they will want to develop skills and interests is really the goal of every dedicated teacher. Bringing more connections with the natural world into children's daily learning can help make this goal a more attainable reality.

Language/Literacy

"A child's quest for knowledge about his world, which is energized by experiences in the outdoors, leads naturally to literacy. Kids have questions, and books have answers. It's really that simple. In the library, a display of books about birds, positioned near a window overlooking bird feeders, shows children how to get the information they crave; the books seem to fly off the shelf. And it works in reverse as well. A child who enjoys the tale of Peter Rabbit will be entranced by planting his own carrots — by living the story. It's a beautiful, continuous loop of discovery that reading makes possible."

Vicky Stever, Director, Hurlburt Field Library
Hurlburt Air Force Base, Hurlburt Field, FL

When children enjoy regular time with teachers and friends in nature-filled outdoor classrooms, language and literacy learning can flourish in deeply meaningful ways. In developmentally appropriate practice it has long been recognized that early language development provides the foundation for later learning in all curriculum areas. It is equally important to recognize that literacy development is about much more than learning a set of symbols (alphabet); it is a system for communicating and making meaning. The stories throughout this section provide great examples of nature's ability to inspire children to want to communicate. You'll notice we have sorted our stories into three categories: Spoken/Body Expression; Written Expression; and Reading/Knowledge of Books. Of course, all of these categories overlap and support each other. And, within each category, you'll see how nature inspires ever-more complex communications as children grow from early childhood into their elementary school years.

Infants and Toddlers

Infants and toddlers who get to spend daily time in outdoor classrooms are naturally motivated to make connections with others. As they use all their senses to interact with the interesting, ever-changing array of natural materials available for in-depth exploration, children will want to ask questions and practice new vocabulary. When caring adults support this natural curiosity and sense of wonder, relationships blossom. Nature continues to provide exciting new opportunities that inspire young children's language development and desire to communicate.

Preschool Children

As preschool children grow, their explorations become more sophisticated. For example, three- and four-year-olds may be inspired to look very closely at the beautiful shapes and textures found in leaves, flowers or bark so they can identify similarities and differences and begin to recognize patterns. Teachers who support this kind of exploration realize children are practicing important skills which are foundational for later development of reading and writing abilities. And interesting real-life experiences in nature continue to inspire ever more complex vocabulary development.

Elementary School Children

Children in elementary grades can practice their growing literacy skills through "real work" in the outdoor classroom. They might use books as references to help identify insects, write signs for the garden, or create poetry inspired by nature's beauty. Opportunities for projects and in-depth study encourage authentic conversation and rich vocabulary development. Nature-filled outdoor classrooms provide a setting in which these projects can happen spontaneously, encouraging interactions where children are talked with more than talked to.

Language/Literacy

Spoken/Body Expression

"The quantity and complexity of children's vocabulary is one of the strongest predictors of reading comprehension." (Smith, 1997)

In outdoor classrooms, young children's rich vocabulary development is readily supported because experiences are first hand and real. Children's inquisitive dispositions lead them to constantly seek new information, and interactions in nature-filled settings allow adults to easily extend children's experiences and thought processes. Lev Vygotsky calls this "scaffolding" children's thinking. (Vygotsky, 1962) In her book, *Mind in the Making*, Ellen Galinsky calls this interaction a "dance." (Galinsky, 2010)

In the early months of life, adults scaffold by talking a lot to babies. They provide a relationship-based spoken language model which is very powerful, especially when it is paired with non-verbal communication such as turn-taking, shared gaze, smiles, and gestures. Nature-filled outdoor spaces provide a lovely venue for these kinds of interactions.

Whispering Winds
Hannah, 3 months

Hannah and I danced out the door to our outdoor classroom today. The wind made me feel like swaying as I carried her, and as I sang to her softly about the wind her eyes lit up. When we got inside the Nature Explore Classroom, I laid Hannah on a blanket near a tuft of tall grass. One particular seed head moved in the wind and curved into her visual field. Hannah looked at the grass intently for almost a minute. She then looked towards me. I said to her, "The grass moves in the wind." Just then a toddler played a few notes on the marimba. I asked, "Did you hear the marimba?" Hannah responded, moving her body, starting from her toes and up to her head in an "s" shape. She smiled and looked at me. She seemed to me to be very pleased. I said the word "marimba" again and she responded in the very same way.

Heather Fox, Infant Teacher
Dimensions Early Education Programs, Lincoln, NE

Insights:

The gentle way the natural world can stimulate senses and heighten children's awareness created a golden opportunity for this joyful contact and rich communication between a caring adult and a very receptive infant. This kind of sensory engagement with nature happens spontaneously in outdoor environments that have been thoughtfully designed. Compare this with many infant environments that are filled almost exclusively with static plastic materials, where experience is artificially created and motivation needs to be manufactured from outward sources.

As infants grow into toddlers, new forms of communication skills emerge. Toddlers learn they can share something they are experiencing with someone else, and realize that spoken words, sign language and gestures can be symbols for thoughts. Consider this story about a toddler who communicated what he was thinking and experiencing to his teacher and friends. The connection with nature provided something important he wanted to communicate.

Cody Knows Crows
Cody, 31 months

While Cody and I were playing on the stump jumpers in the Climbing and Crawling Area of our Nature Explore Classroom, I heard a helicopter in the sky getting louder and louder. As I heard it getting closer, Cody started making the sign-language symbol for "bird" with his fingers. I asked him, "Is that for a helicopter?" Cody said, "No, crow!" I listened again and heard a crow cawing as well. The bird came into view and Cody said, "Caw, caw" while repeating the sign. We had been learning the song "One Little Owl" in which we sang and signed about animals in a tree, including a crow. Cody showed me he was listening more closely than I was and clearly communicated the concept of crow even though I didn't know he had actually seen one. Inside I never would have realized he had internalized this concept and it gave us something fun to talk about. Later that afternoon we grinned at each other when a group of children again sang about the crow!

Nicole Carl, Toddler Teacher
Dimensions Early Education Programs, Lincoln, NE

Insights:

In this story Cody used several ways (sign and spoken language) to communicate his message as clearly as he could. Because this happened outdoors in a "real life" setting, Cody's teacher had the context that allowed her to understand Cody's complete message. How rewarding for Cody that he could show off his skill at sign language and that he could help his teacher see something she might have missed otherwise. After this warm, shared experience, Cody will be more likely to initiate future conversations with his teacher and others.

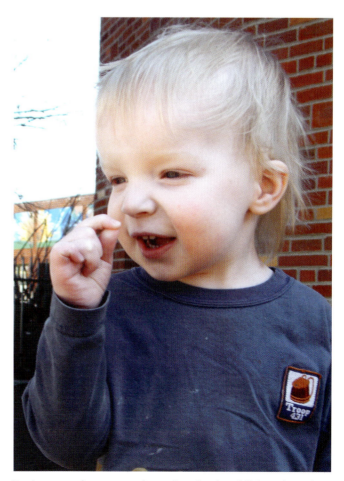

Seeing a real crow outdoors inspired a child to show his teacher that he knew the sign language symbol for crow.

Language/Literacy

Spoken/Body Expression

As children's communication attempts are met with positive responses from adults and peers, their spoken language becomes more complex. In the story below, the sensory experiences provided in an outdoor classroom encouraged children's rich and imaginative use of language.

It Tastes Green
Ellora, age 3 and Andrew, age 5

Ellora and Andrew were in the greenhouse with me when Andrew looked at the potted beets and said, "You can pull that out and eat the bottom." I asked, "If that's the bottom of the beet plant, what's it called?" Andrew paused and said, "Root." Ellora and Andrew then wanted to taste the beet, which wasn't fully grown yet. I helped them taste the beet greens by taking a leaf off the plant and rinsing it. Ellora chewed it and said, "It tastes the same color it is." I asked, "It tastes green?" Ellora responded "Yes!" and we both agreed that some foods do taste green! Together we documented the experience with Ellora cutting a photo of beets from a seed catalog and gluing it on paper. Then with my help she wrote, "I tasted beet greens. They tasted green." She took the paper home to share with her parents after I copied it for her portfolio.

Holly Murdoch, Preschool Teacher
Dimensions Early Education Programs
Lincoln, NE

In addition to the complexity of language that outdoor experiences encourage, many of the stories teachers sent in also contain examples of beautiful, imaginative phrasing and poetic words inspired by nature. Consider this example:

Swinging
Preschool child

A three-year-old was swinging on a swing alongside me. She had closed her eyes, and when she opened them, she said,

"Wow…It's bluer than I imagined it would be. When I close my eyes the sky is bluer than I imagined it when I open them again."

Kimberly Ryan, Preschool Teacher
Child Educational Center
La Canada, CA

Here's an example of how open-ended natural materials can inspire children to engage in storytelling as they weave their own imagination into familiar story lines.

Snow White and the Witch
Three children, age 3

I watched and listened as a small group of children were playing their version of Snow White in our Nature Explore Classroom. Their play consisted of making a "poison" for the "witch." To do this, children piled wood chips, sticks, rocks, bowls, containers and a doll on the ground. Each child contributed to the pile of "poison." As they worked to collect items and add them to the pile they narrated their play.

First child: "A witch is here! A witch is here, Angela!"

Second child: "A witch is here. Terrible, terrible, terrible things."

Third child: "Here is a giant rock to put here. We need some of those rocks to make the witch sneeze."

Michelle Heywood, Preschool Teacher
Child Educational Center
La Canada, CA

Insights:
As children added their own interpretation to a traditional story, they had the chance to be "in control" of a frightening idea…coming into contact with a witch. With a variety of open-ended natural materials readily available and enough space to work without worrying about "making a mess," outdoor settings encourage children to engage in this age-old art of storytelling.

Children at Dimensions Early Education Programs enjoy imaginative play with natural materials.

Language/Literacy

Spoken/Body Expression

Many of the stories we received from folks around the country commented on how successful children with special needs could be in an outdoor classroom. This is true of Jason, in the following story.

Participate and Communicate
Jason, age 4

Jason, diagnosed with autism, rarely spoke or interacted with other children at the beginning of the school year. After two months he was able to engage in his first two-sided conversation with me and a classmate while digging in the sand box on our outdoor classroom. He also established eye contact more readily when engaged outdoors as compared to the indoor classroom. Later in the year Jason was able to direct the actions of a peer, again while involved in a digging activity using dirt and water. While placing water and dirt in a pattern he told a classmate: "Put it here, put water here."

Sherry Pratt, Preschool Teacher
Forest Lake Family Center, Forest Lake, MN

Insights:

When talking about this documentation, Jason's teacher noted that indoors Jason would sometimes sit facing a wall and corner. If he were asked to play, read or participate he usually said "no." Outdoors, where there are more choices and no walls, Jason seemed more able to move about, participate and communicate. Jason's language skills consistently progressed to higher levels whenever he spent time in the outdoor classroom. This confirmed for his teacher that accessibility to the outdoor classroom needs to be seen as much more than a once-in-awhile "bonus." Jason's experience shows that daily access to learning time outdoors is essential.

As children grow older, the outdoor classroom provides an opportunity for ever-more-sophisticated self-expression. In the following story, one elementary school art specialist described how she helped her students thoughtfully express themselves as they used spoken communication, writing and sketching as tools to enhance close observation.

Exploring and Sharing Nature
Elementary school children

In the indoor classroom, my students talk about our five senses. We look at landscape photographs and paintings and pretend we enter them. Students brainstorm words to describe what they might see, hear, smell, taste, and touch if they were inside the nature image. Then we go to our Nature Explore Classroom, clipboards and pencils in hand, to explore a real-life natural space using all of our senses. We record facts about our experience, using words and sketches on paper.

Upon finishing, we gather in the Open Area on our grassy hill and each student is encouraged to share their findings.

Stephanie Carlson-Pruch, Elementary Art Specialist
Gomez Heritage Elementary School, Omaha, NE

Insights:

The process of beginning with two-dimensional art and an imaginary experience, then immersing children in truly sensory opportunities, enhances their word choices and their ability to thoroughly describe the landscapes in their Nature Explore Classroom. Sketching encourages students to look closely; writing descriptive words about smells, textures, and sounds helps children think creatively and develop a richer vocabulary.

Language/Literacy

Written Expression (Symbol Making)

As children's spoken language becomes more sophisticated, they begin to understand that communication can happen through written expression as well. Many activities children engage in on outdoor classrooms can help them develop writing skills. Making maps of their outdoor space, drawing shapes found in nature, or sketching flowers can all be pre-cursers to learning to write letters and words. Interactions with nature often motivate children to want to share what they know with others or record personal discoveries. Wise teachers use this motivation as a way to encourage writing.

Written language is about creating two-dimensional representations of three-dimensional objects and experiences, basically recording something for later use. Children are motivated to learn this form of expression when writing is an integral part of an activity they are physically experiencing. This opportunity happens often in nature-based outdoor classrooms, especially when teachers themselves model the need for written communication as described in the following story.

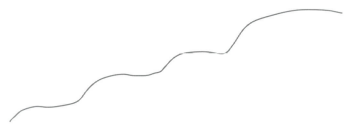

Taking Notes Like a Teacher
Ally, 34 months and Charlotte, age 30 months

I was sitting in the garden with a clipboard taking notes about what the children were doing and saying as they worked with the plants. I told them I wanted to write about their great work. Ally watched me and then came over and told me she wanted to write, too. I gave her my clipboard and pen. She began "writing" with her right hand across the paper in line formation. Ally said, "I am writing my notes down like you did." Seeing all of this, Charlotte came over and asked if she could write her name, too. I got her a new piece of paper and she started with her right hand and then switched to her left. She made wavy lines on the paper, repeatedly switching hands.

Katie Dietz, Toddler Teacher
Dimensions Early Education Programs, Lincoln, NE

Insights:

Ally and Charlotte's teacher, Katie, supported the girls' emerging writing abilities in a number of important ways. First, Katie demonstrated the usefulness of writing as she described how her own written notes would help record the girls' "great work" in the garden. When Ally and Charlotte showed an interest in creating their own writing, Katie knew that it was important to respect these first attempts, and that over time the girls would become interested in learning about letters and words.

In the following story, a calm nature-filled setting encouraged some wonderful writing experiences with preschoolers who were asking about how to form letters.

Writing About Trees
Andrew, age 4 and Ava, age 3

The children and I were lying on the grass with our clipboards, sketching pictures of the trees. One child was especially interested in writing the word "tree" on his sketch, and I worked with him to answer his questions about how to form the letters. I was delighted to see that later when another little girl asked him how to write "tree," he worked with her to support her writing just like I had supported his. He was very patient as he showed her how to make an "R." Sketching pictures of nature often inspires children to want to write words about what they are seeing. And, I think the calm setting we were in made it more possible for children to work together and learn from each other.

Heather Guess, Preschool Teacher
Dimensions Early Education Programs, Lincoln, NE

Being immersed in the natural world often inspires children to want to sketch and write.

Like Andrew and Ava in the previous story, the child in the next story used writing to help record an especially meaningful experience outdoors.

My Marigold
Rory, age 5

Rory came into the greenhouse and wanted to check "my marigold" as he called it. He squirted water in his pot with the sprayer, saying: "It will grow good. It will grow faster." I recalled with him a few days earlier when he had planted three seeds in his pot. Rory went and got paper and pencil and he drew three dots. Next he took the paper and wrote "MARIGOLD" while looking at the writing on the seed packet.

I was thankful we had all these supplies in the greenhouse and Rory knew where to find them, otherwise he probably would not have written about what he was doing. It was clear that the importance of this hands-on experience inspired him to write.

Kris Van Laningham, Preschool Teacher
Dimensions Early Education Programs, Lincoln, NE

Insights:

Rory's teacher has provided support in a number of important ways. She understands that the three dots Rory placed on his paper (to represent the three marigold seeds he planted) are as important to him as the word he writes. By making his three dots, Rory is practicing making meaning through written communication. And, by having writing supplies readily at hand, including a seed packet with the word "marigold" on it, Rory had everything he needed to be able to record his experience when he was "in the moment" and extremely motivated.

Language/Literacy

Written Expression (Symbol Making)

In the following story, a kindergartener was inspired to write during a family nature activity.

Writing with Twig Letters
Zachary, age 6

The plan for our Nature Explore Families' Club activity this month was to collect litter in a local park. Each family was given a collection bag and offered the option of wearing disposable plastic gloves when picking things up. I thought this would be a chance for children to do "real work" and feel empowered to help care for their environment. What I didn't realize was how much this would inspire them to really look closely. Zachary, a kindergartner, proudly exclaimed after just a few minutes, "Look everybody! This stick is one of my letters!" He had found a Y-shaped stick on the ground when reaching for a can, and soon many of the children were excited about looking for "their letters" too. The letter hunt morphed into an alphabet hunt and I was thrilled! I love it when children get excited about what they are doing and it ripples throughout the group. To top it all off, the children began breaking twigs to make the rest of the letters and then several began to write their whole names.

Christine Kiewra, Nature Explore Education Specialist
Dimensions Early Education Programs, Lincoln, NE

Creating letters with sticks inspired children to want to do more writing.

The story below is an example of how nature can motivate a "need to write" in children.

Let's Make a Cook Book
Kennedy, age 4

I was visiting Jewel's Learning Center in Houston, Texas soon after they became a Certified Nature Explore Classroom. I was enjoying a conversation with a number of preschoolers who were telling me about what they wanted to plant in their raised planter beds. One said he wanted to grow cucumbers so he could make pickles. Another talked about wanting tomatoes so she could make salads. Kennedy listened to her friends' comments and turned to me and said: "I want to make a cook book for all the things we grow!" I asked the children how they would make a cook book.

"We'll write it ourselves," they said. Kennedy insisted I write down her great idea and give it to her teacher so it would be sure to happen.

Nancy Rosenow's visit to Jewel's Learning Center
Charlotte Watts, Director, Houston, TX

Nature-filled outdoor classrooms are also great venues for inspiring elementary students to want to write. The next two stories illustrate different writing experiences that the same group of older children enjoyed.

Recording Visual Notes
Elementary school children, grades 2-5

For a number of months, students in my group eagerly made what we called "visual notes" to record their observations of the abundant plant and insect life in our Nature Explore Classroom garden. These notes were a combination of sketches and written words. Equipped with magnifying glasses, clipboards, paper and pencil, the students looked closely, taking their time moving through and pausing in the garden, touching, smelling, and sometimes even tasting plant materials. Students observed carefully, drew sketches, then labeled their sketches of insects and flowers. Sometimes this led to research to determine what kinds of flowers or insects children were finding.

Writing Garden Recipes

One day everyone in our group helped snip fresh rosemary from our garden. We used it to cook a dish which used chick peas, olive oil, spring garlic (also from our garden), salt, pepper and our fresh rosemary. Students were all eager to write the recipe down and take it home. This was a great "real-life reason" for writing!

Holly Murdoch, School-age Teacher
Dimensions Summer Program
Lincoln, NE

Insights:

Just like the preschoolers at Jewel's Center, these older children were motivated to write about things they had grown themselves and were going to enjoy eating. Creating a cook book for garden fare can be a wonderful way to engage students in the writing process.

Language/Literacy

Reading/Knowledge of Books

When children are first learning to read, they seem to use all of their visual ability to essentially "photograph" words, seeing print as a whole. They next begin to understand that words can be broken into parts (letters or graphemes) and that those parts represent spoken sounds (phonemes). As children figure out the process of connecting letters to sounds, experiences in outdoor classrooms can support their understanding of these whole-to-part relationships, which occur in abundance in nature. Experiences in the natural world can also facilitate letter discrimination, which is an important step in developing both reading and writing fluency. Encouraging children to recognize patterns and shapes in nature is an especially effective early reading and writing activity. It is interesting to note, as Ellen Galinsky does in her book, *Mind in the Making*, that all the world's languages have an amazing regularity in the number of times that intersections (like T's, L's and X's) are present in the shapes of letters. Fascinatingly, those shapes with intersections occur at the same rate in natural scenes as they do in written language. So, an activity such as taking young children on an outdoor "shape walk" not only helps them to see patterns in the natural world, it also helps with later letter recognition. Providing natural materials such as twigs and logs (that contain many naturally occurring shapes) is also a great way to help children think about the alphabet.

"Judging from our initial season, the Nature Explorium provides a new and exciting dimension to the library landscape of services. It connects library staff with nature literacy and environmental concerns and engages children in exploration, discovery, and multisensory learning. By providing this outdoor area for the community, the library offers a unique way to connect literacy learning and an appreciation for nature as a regular part of the library visit."

Tracy Delgado-LaStella, Coordinator of Youth Services and Sandra Feinberg, Director, Middle Country Public Library, Centereach, NY

Quotes from books are incorporated throughout the Library's outdoor classroom.

Photo (right) Growing Minds Learning Center, Berkey, OH

Reading/Knowledge of Books

Read the story below to learn what these children know about the letter "Y." They used close observation skills to find the letter shape in a log, and then generalized what they know about the letter in a broader context.

Exploring "Y's"
Nathan, Alex, Jayden, all age 4

Three boys were playing in the Messy Materials Area when one noticed a letter "Y" shape in part of the large climbing log.

"Look, a 'Y,'" said Nathan.

"I have a 'Y' in my name," said Jayden.

Alex said (to the teacher), "Hey, I go to the 'Y' with my Daddy."

Nathan said, "Yeah, let's make more 'Y's."

"Let's get some sticks," added Alex.

Jayden watched for awhile, then helped carry some sticks that the boys used to create more 'Y' shapes.

Ruth Endthoff, Preschool Teacher
Forest Lake Family Center
Forest Lake, MN

Insights:

Imagine if Nathan, Alex and Jayden's teacher had only been "supervising" the boys from a distance. She might have missed their conversation, and wouldn't have known about their interest in letter shapes. But, by paying close attention to their play, she noticed important learning was taking place. She now has many choices about how to help take this learning further. She might encourage an interest in finding other letter shapes in nature, or ask the boys to show the rest of the class their "Y" discoveries. She might especially want to talk to the boys' families about this important early literacy conversation so their parents can celebrate how their children are becoming readers!

Language/Literacy

Experiences in nature can often help children connect more deeply with books. Following are two stories about how books can enhance children's experiences in nature.

Caterpillar Salad
Preschool children

After reading Eric Carle's book, *The Very Hungry Caterpillar*, spotting caterpillars on milkweed in our Nature Explore Classroom, and monitoring two chrysalises in our indoor science area, my group was very focused on caterpillars! Brody was especially curious about which plants they liked to eat most, so I decided to build on his questions with a group activity. The children and I moved through the garden pathway pretending to be caterpillars ourselves and I invited children to snip leaves from plants as we paused near the raised garden bed filled with a variety of lettuces. We collected the harvested leaves in a large bowl, washed them, and mixed them together. Next we feasted on our "Caterpillar Salad" of spinach, arugula, and Red Bibb lettuce. There were lots of conversations that mirrored the story format of the book. Hank said, "I ate through 8 leaves." And Brody pretended the leaves were waffles and said, "I am a very hungry caterpillar and I ate through 4 waffles on Saturday." Several parents told me at dismissal time that their children either had not tried or did not like these lettuces before. They were thrilled that everyone tried and enjoyed our healthy snack. The inspiration from the story in the book made quite a difference!

Christine Kiewra, Nature Explore Education Specialist
Dimensions Early Education Programs
Lincoln, NE

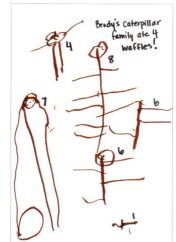

A Yellow Leaf
Emersyn, age 4

"Look, Ms. Jensen, it's the kind of leaf that was in the story," said Emersyn as she brought a big yellow leaf over to me.

"It fell off that tree over there," she added. I was happy to see that Emersyn recalled the pictures from the book I had read called *Leaf Jumpers*.

Barbie Jensen, Preschool Teacher
Dimensions Early Education Programs
Lincoln, NE

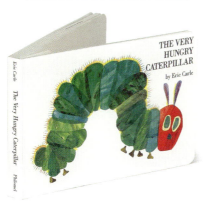

Insights:

Emersyn found meaning in a visual image she had seen in a book, and she was able to hold that powerful mental picture in her head long enough to find a similar image in a leaf on the ground. As Emersyn recalled the story and compared the two-dimensional picture with the three-dimensional leaf, she was able to connect books and real-life experiences in a rich and meaningful way. Her teacher, because she has observed this happening, can now make Emersyn's learning visible for her parents and other adults.

Language/Literacy

Reading/Knowledge of Books

In the following story, nature inspired a child to find a very important use for a book.

Red-Tailed Hawk
Pete, age 4

Pete and several other children noticed a large bird on a rooftop within easy sight from our outdoor classroom. This was interesting to me since we are in a downtown urban setting. Pete came running to tell me, "It's gigantic and it's stepping on something!" The bird was feasting on a pigeon, but this didn't seem to bother the preschoolers. Another teacher, seeing how curious the children were, retrieved some bird books and field guides from indoors and Pete began looking through them. When he got to a page with a Red-Tailed Hawk, I asked if he thought that was the kind of bird we were looking at. Pete wasn't sure because he couldn't see the back of the bird. Comparing the real bird to the picture in the book, we talked about the similarities and differences. As if on cue, the bird turned around and showed his tail. Pete excitedly exclaimed, "It is the Red-Tail Hawk! I see his red tail!" He carried the book around the rest of the morning and announced to anyone who would listen, "I am going to be spending a lot of time with this book!"

Sherry Miller, Preschool Teacher
Dimensions Early Education Programs, Lincoln, NE

Insights:

Pete's teacher wrote that his interest in the Peterson Field Guide of Birds continued. Pete's parents said he became the bird expert at home. They purchased the book for him, helped him start a feather collection, and he tells them often that he has "hawk eyes" and notices details the rest of the family misses. To extend children's interest in the hawk, a local bird expert was invited to visit and bring mounted birds, sketches, and more bird books. Because of this real-life nature experience, children began learning to use non-fiction books as references to fuel their own learning.

Knowing the value of connecting books and nature, the Library Director at Hurlburt Air Force Base came up with a wonderful idea.

Activity Kits at Libraries

We created activity kits for parents and caregivers to check out from the Children's Room of the library and then take out to our Nature Explore Classroom. In each backpack kit is a story, a Nature Explore Families' Club activity sheet, a few other supplies (like a magnifying glass) and sometimes interesting props. We did this to encourage literacy and meaningful interactions between parents and children. These are easy for children to carry and it's a fun way to get more families reading together outdoors!

Vicky Stever,
Director of Hurlburt Field Library
Hurlburt Air Force Base, FL

The entry sign at Hurlburt Library's Certified Nature Explore Classroom invites exploration.

Debra Brownson from St. Ambrose University Children's Campus in Davenport, Iowa, powerfully describes the added value of nature in promoting language and literacy learning:

Could This Have Happened Indoors?

By no means is the question whether literacy learning would or would not happen indoors or outdoors, but more what the outdoors brings to the learning experience — freedom, sun, shade, wind, birds, spiders…For example, you could read the book, *It Looked Like Spilt Milk* (which is about clouds) indoors, or you could read it outside in the grass as children lie on their backs and look up at the sky. The two experiences cannot be compared. When we read outdoors recently, the children were so into the experience that they wanted the book read three times. They then sketched the clouds, labeled the clouds, photographed the clouds, wrote books about the clouds (both the shapes of and later the kinds of). Children shared their books with other classrooms and their families to the point that the books became worn out. Could this have happened indoors? Maybe, but does it? No.

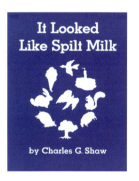

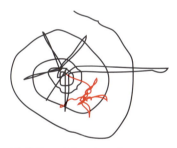

Child's spider drawing

Another example is our spiders. They come in early summer to the bushes on our Nature Explore Classroom. They weave webs on the top of the bushes. The children know this, remember this, look for this. Once the first web is discovered, the children go into a full learning experience as they observe the webs multiply, hope to see spiders, sketch the webs, label the webs, name the spiders, share the "spider bushes" with others, including their families. Could they learn about spiders and the literacy piece indoors? Yes. Could they learn to look forward to nature's wonder each year? Could they focus and study so intently? Would they tie their learning so directly to literacy? Probably not.

From Dimensions Foundation Research

Excerpts from *Young children develop foundational skills through child-initiated experiences in a Nature Explore Classroom: A single case study in La Canada, California* by Ellen Veselack, Lisa Cain-Chang and Dana L. Miller, 2011.

- We identified several language/literacy skills children were developing as they interacted in the Nature Explore Classroom (97% illustrated these skills). Children used complex sentences to communicate ideas and tell their stories. There was a poetic nature to some of the dialogue, and it was rich in imagination. Children also noticed and used print as a way to learn/process information and communicate with others.

- In addition to the complexity of the language children used, children engaged in poetic or imaginative phrasing. These rich images that children described are manifestations of the ways in which experiences with nature influence and enrich children's language skills.

- Children were also highly motivated to "read", based on their initiation of activities that interested them, such as carefully examining plant stakes to learn the names of the plants that were growing in the raised planter beds, or examining books teachers intentionally placed on the table in the garden area.

- Our findings suggest that the Nature Explore Classroom provides a language-rich environment for children to engage with peers, teachers and other adults...The richness of the environment gave children so much to talk about with others. They shared joy in their discoveries, told stories, asked questions, shared information, and often processed their thoughts aloud.

Excerpts from *This never would have happened indoors: Supporting preschool-age children's learning in a Nature Explore Classroom in Minnesota* by Vicki Bohling, Cindy Saarela and Dana L. Miller, 2011.

- Though the majority of play was child-driven, the data also provide excellent examples of teachers supporting children's learning through inquiry, scaffolding and structured activities. These activities were often an opportunity to add experiential learning to concept learning begun in the indoor classroom. This was most commonly accomplished in one of two ways; adding enriching materials and/or guiding observation. For example, the teacher in the "Changing Seasons" nature note supplied children with books, clipboards, paper, and pencils to further the discussion about fall changes that began indoors (Matlon, M. Nature Notes: October 2009). Within this context the children were encouraged to use materials in any way they chose, transferring the power of the learning experience back to the child learners.

- Young children are instinctually drawn to learning that is concrete, experiential and touched by whimsy. The role of materials cannot be underestimated when creating an environment to support and encourage creative, authentic learning. The basic, un-prescribed qualities of natural items such as sticks and dirt require children to make "something of nothing". The limits to learning are restricted only by the depth of the child's own imagination and resourcefulness. This is the very essence of the critical thinking skills which are highly valued yet elusive in education today.

The Dimensions research approach is primarily qualitative action research and currently focuses on exploring the skills children develop through their regular interactions with the natural world. Dimensions Early Education Programs serve as primary research classrooms. Teachers, as co-researchers, and a cadre of national consultants, have been collecting and analyzing data based on direct observations of children since 1998. Secondary research sites for data collection and analysis have also been developed in California and Minnesota. To learn more about our research approach go to dimensionsfoundation.org/research/approach.

 To read the complete papers, go to dimensionsfoundation.org/research.

Science

"Children's early outdoor explorations provide a concrete foundation for the progressive development of major science concepts in the later grades. When these science experiences focus on science processes (such as observation and analysis), children have the opportunity to develop scientific understandings that are far more important than right answers.

Importantly, outdoor play enables children's natural curiosities and develops essential attitudes toward learning. This play may be viewed as the highest form of research!"

Julie Thomas, Ph.D.
Frank and Carol Morsani Endowed Chair of Science Education, Oklahoma State University

In the last generation, outdoor settings for children have become increasingly sanitized, rubberized spaces devoid of nature's "loose parts" that invite the kinds of hands-on discovery that supports science learning. And, as children have begun spending more out-of-school-time in front of screens instead of exploring nature, their understanding of the world around them is coming more from media instead of from direct observation, leaving lots of room for misconceptions to develop. It's typical for today's children to know more about the rainforest or arctic regions of the world than what's in their own backyards or neighborhoods.

Nature-based outdoor spaces in early childhood programs, elementary schools, and in places where families spend time, are once again giving children access to daily explorations in nature. These in-depth, personal experiences provide a sensory basis for developing deeply meaningful and foundational science understandings.

Just as all learning is on a continuum, science learning begins as an infant develops basic understandings and intuitive comprehension about the natural world, then becomes ever more complex and comprehensive from early childhood to young adulthood. By their very nature, all young children are scientists. They have a natural curiosity and the world is their laboratory. In a nature classroom, children are observing, investigating, devising experiments, problem-solving and, through that process, learning scientific concepts even before they have the scientific vocabulary. As children's language development matures, they are later able to attach vocabulary to what they know intuitively.

As we studied the stories sent to us about science learning in Nature Explore Classrooms, we were able to group them into five categories of understandings and experiences including: Cause and Effect; Close Observation; Cycles and Seasons; Classification; and Environmental Awareness.

"It is a wholesome and necessary thing for us to turn again to the Earth, and in the contemplation of her beauties to know of wonder and humility."
Rachel Carson, *The Sense of Wonder*

"What do parents owe their young that is more important than a warm and trusting connection to the Earth?"
Theodore Roszak, *The Voice of the Earth*

Cause and Effect

As young children begin to experience the ability to create reactions to their own actions, they develop an understanding of the concept of "cause and effect." Daily experiences in nature provide a wonderful canvas for exploring how the world works. Nature provides many free "tools" that help young children explore the science principle of cause and effect, as the story below illustrates.

Breaking Sticks
Grayson, age 31 months

Grayson was in the Nature Explore Classroom under a tree. He was picking up different sticks and breaking them. He seemed to be listening to the sound each stick made as he snapped it in two. After a particularly loud sound, he looked up at me and said, "Watch me." I asked him what sound it made. He said, "Loud." He continued to break sticks into various lengths one after another for about 10 minutes.

Katie Dietz, Infant/Toddler Teacher
Dimensions Early Education Programs, Lincoln, NE

Insights:

As Grayson engaged in the simple activity of breaking sticks, he was experiencing his ability to make things happen (cause and effect). He was also learning about the properties of wood and his own strength. There would be no meaningful way for him to gain this information other than through his own actions. Listening closely to the sounds produced as he broke various-sized sticks and experiencing how each stick felt in his hands as it broke provided Grayson with rich sensory information. He now has many "hooks" with which to later recall what he knows about sticks and the physical properties of wood. Grayson was clearly in charge of his own learning. Because his teacher noticed and recorded this exploration, she will now be able to support Grayson's growing knowledge of cause and effect principles, and she can help his family celebrate Grayson's interest in this kind of fundamental "research."

A Breezy Afternoon
Brandon, age 4

On a brisk, breezy afternoon, Brandon was in the outdoor cabin watching the flowing red curtain flutter in the doorway. He caught it as it blew toward him, then let it go. He walked through it and let the fabric glide over his body and head. When the wind died down he took the corners at the bottom and straightened it, then waited for the wind to catch it once again.

Kimberly Ryan, Preschool Teacher
Child Educational Center, La Canada, CA

Insights:

Children's play can seem deceptively simple if we are not paying attention to the important learning that is often occurring. In Brandon's story, his simple actions allowed him to experiment with the cause and effect properties of wind. His teacher wisely documented Brandon's experimentation, knowing that he was discovering foundational science principles.

Water Pathways
Elementary school children, grades 2-5

We took two walking excursions to a nearby creek where the rocky banks are easily accessible. The children were fascinated by the path that the water had carved out of the banks. This became the basis of our water pathways exploration back in our Nature Explore Classroom in the Sand Area and then later in the Messy Area. Some children experimented with releasing water collected in the rain barrel onto the sand to see how it flowed and if it would create a stream. This quickly led to the idea of building channels to get water to travel further and "carry more stuff." This became a study of gravity as well. Children used sections of guttering and chunks of wood to create pathways to pour water down. Madeleine (age nine) had paid close attention to the "humps" and curves in the creek and wanted to replicate them in her pathway. High level thinking and construction and engineering skills were needed to get water to travel the entire length of the pathways and to move with enough velocity to carry woodchips down as well.

Holly Murdoch, School-age Teacher
Dimensions Summer Programs, Lincoln, NE

Insights:

In this story, these older children were still exploring ideas of cause and effect, although in a more sophisticated way. Clearly, many science understandings were being developed concurrently through this child-driven inquiry process. A large Sand Area space that could accommodate long pathways was necessary to allow this rich experimentation to occur.

Science

Close Observation

Dimensions research consistently demonstrates that close observation skills are strengthened when children spend time in Nature Explore Classrooms. The National Science Education Standards developed by the National Academy of Sciences emphasize the importance of supporting children's development of close observation abilities:

"During the first years of school, they should be encouraged to observe closely the objects and materials in their environment, note their properties, distinguish one from another and develop their own explanations of how things become the way they are."

Children who are able to explore the natural world regularly and over time become comfortable seeking new information. As they ask questions, actively explore, compare what they think they know with what they are observing, then reflect on their new assumptions, they become active participants in the process of developing ever-more complex science understandings. This way of learning strengthens critical thinking skills, which is helpful in all areas of learning, not just science.

Investigating Grasshoppers
Preschool child

Lonnie closely observed a grasshopper in the greenhouse. No photograph or story in a book could provide him with the same information he gathered in this hands-on way.

Jenny Leeper Miller, Master Teacher
Ruth Staples Child Development Laboratory
University of Nebraska-Lincoln

As children engage in close observation of the world around them, their sense of wonder grows.

Exploring Spiders
Oskar and Derek, age 4, Levi and George, age 5

"I saw the spider!" said Oskar, spying a large spider on the side of the building. "I need to go get a book to see if we can find one that looks like that." We went to the Science Area and returned with a spider book and magnifying glass. Several children gathered around trying to identify the spider and I gave them clipboards and pencils to encourage them to sketch as well. Derek who was busily sketching and talking to himself said, "one, two, three, four, five, six, seven, eight" apparently counting the legs as he drew them. I told him, "Wow you are a scientist and an artist!" George who was also sketching brought his clipboard to me saying, "Um, this one is the spider on the wall and this one I just drew is a Daddy Long Legs." Children went on to compare the actual spider to the photographs in the books noticing details like "bits of brown and yellow." Then really looking closely, Levi said, "That is where the silk comes out of him!"

Suzan Haley, Preschool Teacher
Dimensions Early Education Programs, Lincoln, NE

Insights:

This teacher understands that encouraging children to document their investigations through sketching strengthens their close observation skills. Much of children's internalized science understandings come from noticing changes, finding patterns, and looking at relationships. Adults who support children's interests and take their investigations seriously help children see themselves as capable, competent science learners. Encouraging on-going documentation of investigations over a long period of time can help children look for patterns or find out new information. This helps children expand their ability to think deeply about how the world works, and it sometimes causes them to reconsider their ideas. Documentation through sketching is also a form of authentic assessment and can be used to celebrate developmental milestones with families. Note that along with literacy learning, Derek was also strengthening mathematical thinking as he counted the legs of the spider.

Falling Feathers
Hailey, age 3

Hailey came to me holding a small black and white pigeon feather in her hand and told me that she was going to give the feather to her mommy. I acknowledged that her mother would like the gift and asked if she knew where the feather came from. Hailey led me to the sandbox and pointed to a spot saying, "It fell right here." I asked where she thought it fell from and Hailey answered, "A feather tree." I pointed to the closest tree and asked if it was the one it fell from. Hailey said she thought so. I pointed to the branches and encouraged her to look closely, asking, "Does this tree have feathers?" She said, "No." I led her to another larger tree nearby and we wondered together if the feather fell from this tree. Hailey said she thought so, but when I asked her if this one had feathers, she again replied, "No. Maybe it just flew over and landed there." I told Hailey I had an idea and pointed to where the pigeons could be seen at the edge of the building. "Do you see the birds up there? The pigeons?" I asked Hailey. One pigeon flew overhead and Hailey excitedly said, "Yes! I see it!" I asked, "Do you know what birds have on their bodies?" Hailey said, "Feathers. To keep them comfy." I waited a few seconds then asked, "Do you think that feather could have fallen from a bird?" Hailey said, "Yes. It came from a kind of pigeon." She observed her feather closely and added, "A white and black pigeon." Hailey walked to the sandbox and I heard her tell Lillias, "This feather came from a white and black pigeon."

Kristi Reitz, Preschool Teacher
Dimensions Early Education Programs, Lincoln, NE

Insights:

Hailey's teacher could have simply told her that feathers came from birds, not trees. Instead, by encouraging the use of close observation skills, this wise teacher made it possible for Hailey to participate in her own learning process. Had her teacher simply corrected her, rather than helping her evaluate and later change her initial thinking, Hailey may not have been willing or able to make the mental shift needed to "accommodate" new information. This real-time nature exploration helped Hailey strengthen her self-image as a learner while allowing her to develop a new science understanding. Hailey was even able to use her new knowledge to teach her friend.

Shade vs. Sun
Graceyn, age 5

This Child Observation Form documents how close observation of a group of two different plants, one in the shade and one in the sun, led to a child's hypothesis.

Cindy Heinzman, Preschool Teacher
Dimensions Early Education Programs, Lincoln, NE

Child Observation Form – Nature Notes

Teacher/Observer: Cindy Heinzman
Date: 5-3-10

Brief description of activity: Discussion about the bushes at the NEC entrance
Materials/props used: bushes in the pots
Why you believe this is significant: close observation, noticing differences, cause & effect

Child(ren): Graceyn A. Age/Birthdate: 5/4-15-05 Gender: F

Time of Day/Location: 12:45 NEC entrance

Location of Activity
- ☐ Climbing/Crawling area
- ☐ Messy Materials area
- ☐ Building area
- ☐ Nature Art area
- ☐ Garden/Pathways
- ☐ Greenhouse
- ☐ Music/Movement area
- ☐ Open area
- ☐ Gathering area
- ☐ Dirt Digging area
- ☐ Sand area *NEC Entrance*
- ☐ Brick Wall

Resources
- ☐ Akambira
- ☐ Nature Art Table
- ☐ Tree Cookies
- ☐ Tree Blocks
- ☐ Square/Rectangle Blocks
- ☐ Rainstick
- ☐ Scarves
- ☐ Garden Tools
- ☐ Clipboards
- ☐ Magnifying Glasses
- ☐ Nature Image Cards
- ☐ Nature Image Posters
- ☐ Tape Measures
- ☒ Other: bushes in pots

As we approached the NEC today, we stopped to notice the two bushes at the entrance. The bush in the pot to the north had lots of leaves, but the one to the south had hardly any, but did have many buds. We talked as a group for a little bit and then I said, "I wonder why they look so different?"

Graceyn said, "That one is in the shade and this one is in the sun."

(side of the building blocks the sun)
(shade) N → (sun)
Entrance to NEC

Insights:

By making close observations of the world around them part of daily class routines, this preschool group was able to notice changes over time. Graceyn now knows that plants need sunlight to grow, and she understands the appropriate amount of sunlight needed for their optimal development. Without regular time in nature, children aren't able to personally observe the cycles of life and develop deep, intuitive understandings from personal experiences. As language abilities and more refined motor skills develop, children are able to engage their curiosity and sense of wonder in a variety of ways. They become more and more comfortable with asking questions and are capable of seeking their own answers.

Science

The following story illustrates how a simple outdoor experience provided an opportunity for an investigation.

Investigating Ants
Preschool children

In the warmer weather we often spend our entire day outside in our outdoor classroom, including during our lunchtime. Children gather in different areas throughout the yard and we have picnic lunches. One day a small group of children decided to eat under one of our larger trees and they were ambushed by ants. As they got up to move, one of the children left behind a small piece of bread. The ants, of course, took the bread and began to carry it away. This led to an investigation. Another child dropped a piece of fruit, and then there was a cracker, and then some carrots…everyone wanted to leave something for the ants. We decided to do some research about ants and the class came up with a "menu" for our newfound friends. Under the tree we placed small bowls with different foods and we charted what the ants took. The children were so amazed at how fast the bowls emptied!

Nancy Salerno, Director
Growing Minds Learning Center, Berkey, OH

Insights:

Children were successful in using the scientific inquiry method with minimal teacher scaffolding. Probably the most important way this wise teacher supported children was by providing them the time outdoors to investigate. Her recognition of the children's own interests validated their important research.

Opportunities for Observation
Elementary school children

I use our outdoor classroom to examine ecosystems, study plant types, and with sixth graders to study plant reproduction. We chose to plant both deciduous and evergreen trees in our space so the students can see reproduction in flowering as well as cone-bearing trees. When we study monocot and dicot plants, we observe identifiable characteristics of both in the leaves, flowers, and roots. Often after the activity is complete, students return to the outdoor classroom and conduct their own investigations on the topics that most interested them.

Nancy Curry, Science Teacher
Blue Hill Elementary School, Blue Hill, NE

Insights:

Practicing close observation skills helps children develop increasingly higher and more abstract cognitive abilities. And, providing regular opportunities

for children to believe in their own investigative abilities encourages them to define themselves as lifelong learners. In Nature Explore Classrooms, opportunities also regularly present themselves for children to experience and study first-hand the Earth's systems, such as seasons and the life cycles of plants and animals.

The following story was sent in by an educator who hosts elementary students as they visit her Nature Explore Classroom on field trips. It reminds us that not all students are yet able to grow up with nature exploration as a part of their daily lives.

The Value of Personal Exploration
Elementary school children

In the woods portion of our outdoor classroom, we were on the nature trail and I was leading a group of elementary age "city kids" who were visiting on a field trip. I asked the children to identify a type of fungus, and the child I called on said, "Athlete's foot!" This led to some chuckles and a whole lot of discussion along the path. The students were curiously examining all the fungi and coming up with clever guesses about what they were actually named. On another field trip soon after, many children were hesitant to get dirty. One child even had brought gloves and wouldn't take them off the whole time he was at the farm. We had all the kids get in a circle in the field, reach down and grab a handful of dirt, and just rub it between their hands. Many said this was the first time they had ever had a handful of dirt!

Linda Grinthal, Director
Sunset View Farm, Lafayette, NJ

Insights:

These children, who hadn't had much experience in nature, clearly benefitted from the opportunity to get their hands dirty, explore dirt and brainstorm ideas for plant names. Compare the lack of experience and information the older children in the story above had with what the young toddler, Kathy, on the next page learned through her own observational skills with the help of the thoughtful scaffolding from her teacher.

Science

Cycles and Seasons

"As children observe, reflect, record, and share nature's patterns and rhythms, they are participating in a process that promotes scientific and ecological awareness, problem solving, and creativity." (Hensley, 2006)

Carefully choosing plants for your outdoor classroom that will provide a variety of scents, colors, textures and blooming patterns throughout the year will give children a firsthand opportunity to observe life cycles. Involving children in plant care will not only bring benefits for science learning, but will also help them take initial steps toward a lifetime of environmental stewardship. The toddler in the following story was beginning her journey.

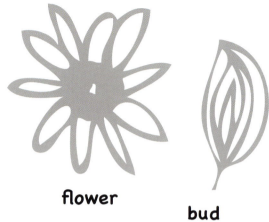
flower   bud

I'm Watering the Plant!
Kathy, age 34 months

I noticed Kathy at the drinking fountain, holding an uprooted plant in her hand. I asked her what she was doing and Kathy innocently answered, "I'm watering the plant!" I grinned and explained that the plant needed to stay in the ground but suggested that we could use a watering can to bring the water to the plant. We walked to the garden and found where Kathy had taken the plant out of the soil. Together we put the plant back in the ground and gently patted the earth around it. I then asked Kathy to touch the soil and tell me if it felt wet or dry. Kathy told me it felt wet, so we decided this plant didn't need more water right now. We went in search of a garden bed that felt dry and needed water. Together we filled the watering can and Kathy watered that bed.

Shannon Walsh, Preschool Teacher
Child Educational Center, La Canada, CA

Insights:
Kathy was learning to be a caretaker for the plants in her Nature Explore Classroom; she just needed a little coaching on how to best care for them! Her gentle and insightful teacher taught Kathy not only how to water plants but also how to decide for herself if they need additional water.

Read the story below to see how a preschooler's close observation skills and plant knowledge have evolved beyond the toddler-level of understanding.

From Bud to Flower
Charlene and Rachel, age 4

While exploring the garden, Rachel reached down, picked up a flower and ran to tell me, "This flower fell on the ground, but I think I found the plant it fell from!" Rachel and I walked back to the garden and confirmed that the single flower she had found came from the plant she identified. Rachel's friend Charlene then opened her hand to reveal a flower bud. Rachel examined the bud and explained to her friend that she had a "flower" from the same plant from which Charlene had the "bud."

Kimberly Ryan, Preschool Teacher
Child Educational Center, La Canada, CA

Insights:
Through documenting a simple encounter, this observant teacher learned much about Rachel's scientific understandings. For example, it is clear that Rachel understands that buds and flowers represent two different stages in the growth of the same plant. She was also able to use close observation skills to determine which plant the flower she found had come from.

Photo (right) Gomez Heritage Elementary School, Omaha, NE

Science

In the following story that happened in a Dirt Digging Area, the open-ended properties of dirt allowed Macy to play out a hibernation scenario in which she demonstrated her knowledge of frogs and what they do during cold weather.

Frog Habitat
Macy, age 3

In late fall, before snow cover and cold weather set in, Macy headed directly for the Dirt Digging Area and remained there for the entire time we were outdoors. As she shoveled dirt into a pail she told me that she was making a habitat and I asked her, "Who lives in your habitat?" She quickly replied that it was a habitat for frogs. She continued working, adding leaves to the pail as food for the frogs to eat. When I asked Macy how long the frogs stayed in their habitat, she confidently stated that "they nap for a long, long, long time, all the way to Christmas. When they get up they go out to get a little bit of chocolate." (Macy's mom noted that her daughter wakes up every morning asking if today is Christmas.)

Susan Wilcox, Preschool Teacher
Forest Lake Family Center, Forest Lake, MN

Macy was inspired to make a habitat for her frog.

Insights:

Because of her many experiences in the outdoor classroom, and because of her teacher's ongoing interest and support, Macy understands the meaning of "habitat," and she understands the concept of hibernation, even if she might not know the exact word yet. When children have opportunities to continually explore the natural world, they can build on existing science knowledge, try out new theories about how the world works, and refine those theories as they gain more experience.

Children who explore outdoor classroms in all kinds of weather develop a personal understanding of seasons.

In the story below, it is clear that Korben, also a preschooler, recognized changes in his environment because he has spent time exploring the same space in all kinds of weather.

Understanding Seasons
Korben, age 4

On this March morning it was well above freezing. Former observations of Korben have shown that he has come back time and time again to a particular spot near the greenhouse where he has found snow or ice over the course of the winter. I noticed today that this spot was only covered by water. I brought Korben over and showed him the standing water. I asked him if he remembered what used to be there. Korben replied, "Yeah. Very slippery ice and now it is a puddle." We talked about how today, since it is warmer, the ice had melted.

A few minutes later Korben came to me and said, "Mrs. Reitz, I'm freezing. My hands are freezing. Why is it freezing?" We discussed that even though it was warm enough for ice to melt, it was still cold on our hands. "When is it going to be spring?" Korben asked. "We've been waiting for it to be spring." "How will you know when it's spring?" I asked. Korben said, "All the plants will grow and we'll make our family's garden." He paused, and then said, "The leaves in our yard are starting to grow." He looked up at the branches of a tree. "But our school leaves are not starting to grow."

Kristi Reitz, Preschool Teacher
Dimensions Early Education Programs, Lincoln, NE

Insights:

Knowledge of seasonal changes and their indicators show up throughout this piece of documentation. This skilled teacher helped her student look closely and consider details related to water properties and weather. Through open-ended questions, Korben's teacher learned a lot about what he understands about seasons and the life-cycles of plants.

Science

"The middle years — roughly six to twelve — is a time of greatly expanded interest, curiosity and capacity for assimilating knowledge and understanding the natural world. Rapid cognitive and intellectual growth occurs, including many critical thinking skills achieved through interaction and coping in the nonhuman environment. Intellectual development at this stage is especially facilitated by direct contact with nearby natural settings, where a world of exploration, imagination and discovery becomes increasingly evident to the child."

Stephen R. Kellert, School of Forestry and Environmental Studies, Yale University

In the following story, a group of middle-years students experienced the excitement that comes from watching the cycles of life.

Caterpillars to Butterflies
Elementary school children

Curiosity was contagious as my students, ages six to eight, watched larvae grow into caterpillars. Once the caterpillars were hanging inside their chrysalises, the children waited with anticipation for them to emerge as butterflies. As the days went by, their excitement grew. The awe on their faces was priceless as they witnessed the first Painted Lady slowly climbing out of its chrysalis! The children spent a few days observing the butterflies in our indoor garden. They learned to describe the life cycle of a butterfly and to identify its body parts. They especially enjoyed watching as a butterfly would uncurl its proboscis to sip nectar from a flower. Finally, the big day arrived. It was time to release our butterflies outside in our Nature Explore Classroom. With mixed emotions, we headed to our Gathering Area. But as each butterfly soared into the air, the children clapped and shouted with joy! For the next few weeks, each time they spotted a Painted Lady in the garden, they wondered if it was one of their own.

Jean Luchini, Special Education Teacher
Beard School, Chicago, IL

The butterfly study at Beard School was a joyful experience for all.

Classification

From birth, babies use their senses to gather information and make meaning from the chaos that surrounds them. They sort through all of the sensory input they receive, search for patterns and begin to classify what they are observing into various categories. In this way, the world begins to make more sense. This process continues, in ever more sophisticated ways, throughout a child's school years.

In the following story, preschool children are deciding how to classify materials they are using. Their task becomes even more challenging with the added social complexity of differing perspectives.

What is Nature?
Preschool children

Harriet found a rock and announced, "This is my special rock." She carried it around, and then placed the rock on the ground, announcing: "I can put this rock here because it's nature." Upon hearing this, Patrick ran over, picked up the rock and corrected her: "Actually, Harriet, that's not really part of nature, it's a rock." Hearing this exchange I interjected with an open-ended question, "What is a rock if it's not a part of nature?" Patrick quickly replied, "It's from the ground." I wondered aloud again, "What is nature?" Patrick answered, "Tigers are nature. Lions are nature." Harriet countered with, "No. Nature is plants." Patrick told her, "Animals are nature." Harriet repeated, "Nature is plants." Patrick acquiesced and said, "Plants are nature. Animals are nature. Blue whales are the largest animal. Bigger than a T-rex." Harriet said, "I know that!"

Susan Walsh, Preschool Teacher
Child Educational Center, La Canada, CA

Insights:

Allowing children to create and debate their own theories of how the world works is a great strategy for supporting their sense of themselves as capable science learners. Notice how the teacher in the story used open-ended questions to keep providing the children a chance to debate their understandings of what it means for something to be classified as "nature."

Science

The story below provides a wonderful example of the complex classification skills children needed to use as they predicted the kinds of food a snake might eat.

The Snake Story
Preschool children

The children noticed a snake moving in the back of the flower garden along the edge of the building. A teacher nearby, Tina, was able to gently catch the snake so the children could examine it more closely. The children were fascinated to see the snake at their school. They wanted to study the snake further. The next day Tina brought in a fish aquarium to make a temporary home for the snake. The children talked about what living things need to live and grow and what the snake would need to live in its temporary home. They gathered leaves and grass to make the snake comfortable in the aquarium. Then they asked, "What do snakes eat?" The children had their own ideas about what a snake might eat. During Morning Meeting, the group reviewed a list of all the snake-eating predictions the children had made the day before. The group discussed ways to observe what types of food the snake would eat. The children and teachers then went outside to collect the items on the food list. The children tested their predictions by placing the items in the aquarium with the snake. They watched and watched as the snake found the worm wiggling in the grass and then ate it whole! They continued to watch and watch and the snake did not eat any of the other food items in the aquarium. The next day the children put another worm in the aquarium and the snake quickly ate it up. The previous day's conclusion was confirmed. Snakes eat worms.

Christine Davidson, Early Childhood Teacher
Center for Early Education and Care
University of Massachusetts Amherst
Amherst, MA

Insights: (provided by Judy Harris Helm):

This snake experience was well documented through photographs, the collection of the children's chart on predicted foods and the narrative by the teacher. It became a storybook that children could read in the book area and parents could check out to read at home. The documentation enabled teachers, parents, and others to reflect on what children learned and the effectiveness of the experience. The documentation also revealed the ability of children to stay focused, set up an investigation, and follow through to form their own conclusion. These are valuable executive functioning skills which contribute to school achievement.

As is often the case in learning experiences which emerge spontaneously in rich outdoor environments, the children's intense interest in natural phenomena engaged and motivated them to use higher level thinking skills than ones they needed to use to do typical preschool tasks such as sorting items by color. Emotional involvement spurs peak performance which is then easily captured for portfolios and assessment checklists. As these children were excitedly involved in capturing the snake, setting up their experiment, and observing, the teacher was able to collect authentic evidence of their knowledge and skills.

Judy Harris Helm, Ed.D., Consultant
Best Practices Inc.
Brimfield, IL

Environmental Awareness

Developmentally appropriate earth science learning can and should also lead to environmental awareness. Helping children develop emotional connections to the natural world is the most appropriate place to begin. Authentic science learning helps children become more knowledgeable about the Earth's systems and the interconnectedness of humans and the natural world.

As Judy Harris Helm and Lilian Katz state in their book, *Young Investigators*:

"One of the goals of increasing children's connection with nature is the development of an attitude of stewardship toward the environment. As children use the project approach to study nature topics in depth, they often become protective of living things. One kindergarten class that was studying a wild area near a park by their school became quite concerned to discover trash littering the area. They worked hard to clean up the trash, and after much discussion, decided to make a poster telling others not to 'throw your stuff here.' This led to making more posters and putting them in other places throughout their community."

A love for the natural world can develop quite early if children are provided with daily opportunities for nature experiences, as is the case in the story below.

Loving the Leaves
Will, age 16 months

Will played in the leaves under a tree on our Nature Classroom. At his young age he was experiencing seasonal and weather changes for the very first time, and he clearly enjoyed the sensory experience. He learned about his environment by being immersed in it. Frequent experiences like this lead to feeling a deep connection with the natural world.

Katie Miller, Director
James R. Russell Child Development Center
Creighton University, Omaha, NE

Insights:

Outdoor classrooms designed specifically for infants and toddlers make it easy for adults to provide children the time and space to discover and interact with all kinds of nature.

Science

Read the next story to see how a teacher and a preschool director helped a child develop a connection to nature by fostering his emotional caretaking abilities.

It's a Living Thing
Toddler children

One of the children pulled down a branch and broke it off the tree. So our director Pepper and I went over to him and we said, "Oh no, it's got a boo-boo. This is a living thing." We took a long time with him. We read a book about it. We brought the branch inside and put it in a vase of water, and it actually bloomed! And every day we would change the water and ask the same child who had broken it off to put in more water. So the next time we went outside, he was telling all the other kids pulling the leaves off, "No, no, no, it's a living thing. It's a living thing." So he understood that the tree was a living thing that was hurt when he pulled off the branch. I believe he was around two years and four months. I remember, I did an observation on it because it was just amazing to see him have a connection. And then we actually walked around outside, and I told him that it's the same for bushes and for the trees in the back and for the grass. It was nice to see the emotional connection he had with the living things outside.

Sandra Beltran, Toddler Teacher
Five Towns Early Learning Center, Inwood, NY

Insights:

These caring adults were able to turn a negative situation into a positive learning opportunity that is likely to stay with this child for a long time. Had they chosen to focus on the child's negative behavior through shaming or punishment, neither the tree nor the child would have grown.

The importance of joyful playtime outdoors, even for older children and adults, can be easily forgotten but should not be discounted. As Rachel Carson said, "For the child… it is not half so important to know as to feel. If facts are the seeds that later produce knowledge and wisdom, then the emotions and the impressions of the senses are the fertile soil in which the seeds must grow…It is more important to pave the way for a child to want to know than to put him on a diet of facts that he is not ready to assimilate."

Read below to see how an adult's attitude helped two preschoolers grow in their love of the natural world.

Lovable Slugs
Avery and Catrice, age 4

Avery found a slug under a tree cookie outside in the Messy Materials Area and studied it. I helped her get the slug to crawl on a leaf so she could look at it more closely. She did not want to hold it in her hand, but she felt  comfortable holding the leaf and observing the slug. "Do they bite?" Avery asked. I assured her no and she relaxed and said, "Look, it curled up like a ball, like a roly-poly. Look at its trail on the leaf!" Catrice came over to see what was going on. Catrice was much more comfortable with the slug and asked Avery if she could hold it. Catrice said, "I found a slug in my backyard before. Once I found a hundred under a log! This slug is so slimy. I love it! It's so pretty, I could almost kiss it!"

Cindy Heinzman, Preschool Teacher
Dimensions Early Education Programs, Lincoln, NE

Insights:

With the support of a caring teacher, Avery learned about more than slugs. She was able to increase her comfort level with something unfamiliar and potentially frightening to her. This might not have happened if her teacher had either shown displeasure herself or insisted Avery hold the slug in her hand. Once comfortable, Avery became curious and found the slug interesting, even comparing it to another insect with which she was more familiar.

In the story below, a group of older students and their teacher benefitted from a chance to play in nature!

The Good Life
Elementary school children

I was doing a three-week Saturday school with 3rd and 4th graders using our outdoor classroom. I began our first session by asking the children, "What is nature?" and "What things affect nature?" Next we went outside in the 20-degree weather, with snow and no wind, and we played! We had a huge snowball fight and a run fest. It was so fun! Then we went to the Gathering Area, stood on stumps, and talked about our favorite part of the snowfest. This led to really meaningful discussions about what the students can do to help or protect nature in their own outdoor classroom that means so much to them. We made and signed a group pledge to recycle, clean up after ourselves, plant flowers and trees. We will add to this as we go on. Ahh! Life is good!

Stephanie Carlson-Pruch, Elementary Art Specialist
Gomez Heritage Elementary School, Omaha, NE

Insights:

Having had a chance to experience the fun of being in nature, students were motivated and ready to discuss ways to care for nature.

The story below speaks eloquently about the ability of time in nature to inspire.

Lighting a Spark!
An adult's reflection

The benefit of having our Nature Explore Classroom is immeasurable. My students are able to have free exploration time in a safe outdoor setting designed just for them. Something simple that most adults take for granted (a pile of dead leaves) can lead into a variety of lessons on life cycles, habitats, living things, and seasons. It even crosses the curriculum into math (measuring and sorting) and social studies (how cultures use trees and other plants). The time in nature my young students are receiving is lighting that spark of respect and passion for the natural world that will stay with them for the rest of their lives. On a personal side note: As a child, I was busy exploring and making new discoveries in my backyard, which sparked my interest in nature and led to my career as a zookeeper (I worked in the predator departments at Zoo Atlanta and the Birmingham Zoo) and ultimately as a science teacher. I am a kinesthetic learner, which is why I believe I benefited from learning in nature so much as a child, and why I teach the way I do. Without having my Nature Explore Classroom, I wouldn't be able to teach to my fullest potential, so not only do the children benefit from it, but as an adult, I do as well.

Elizabeth Beckwith, Science Lab Teacher,
St. Martin's Episcopal School, Atlanta, GA

From Dimensions Foundation Research

Excerpts from *Young children develop foundational skills through child-initiated experiences in a Nature Explore Classroom: A single case study in La Canada, California* by Ellen Veselack, Lisa Cain-Chang and Dana L. Miller, 2011.

- These young scientists explored the Nature Explore Classroom as if it were their laboratory and engaged in scientific discovery. They explored nature and natural habitats, and examined various properties of the items they found…They had opportunities (and time) to pursue their inquiries, and experiment over and over (as Adam did when he balanced branches and planks with a string) until they had satisfied their curiosity.

- Eighty-nine percent of our Nature Notes identified specific science skills children were developing. As children in this study explored the Nature Explore Classroom, they used many of the same skills scientists use. Children observed closely, asked questions, hypothesized, tested their hypotheses, made adjustments and formulated conclusions. They also engaged in debate about their findings with others. They experienced weather firsthand, including rain, thunder, wind, and temperature fluctuation. They experimented with water and learned about flow, pressure, force, and absorption. They physically experienced scientific concepts such as gravity, weight, and cause and effect (cause and effect was most frequently cited – it was identified in 34% of the observations).

Key themes that emerged from this study:

- Many of the science skills children developed centered on learning about nature and often involved telling others what they knew about nature.

- Children's experiences with natural materials included interacting with plants that were intentionally selected and planted in the Nature Explore Classroom. As children encountered plant life, through their close observations they learned to identify plants and also assumed some responsibility for caring for those plants. These encounters with plant life in the Nature Explore Classroom, and discussions about plants, gave children firsthand experiences with natural habitats and opportunities to further develop their knowledge of plant life.

- Children had many opportunities to investigate and physically experience the scientific concepts of gravity and weight as they explored objects and their bodies and physically manipulated materials in the Nature Explore Classroom.

Excerpts from *This never would have happened indoors: Supporting preschool-age children's learning in a Nature Explore Classroom in Minnesota* by Vicki Bohling, Cindy Saarela and Dana L. Miller, 2011.

- Surprisingly, some of the most complex, creative play themes were observed during the winter months when snow covered the ground and some features of the outdoor space were unavailable.

- In the Nature Explore Classroom outdoor play is no longer a time when staff stands back, detached from the action, supervising from a distance. Rather, the outdoor classroom becomes a purposeful space for teaching and learning across the curriculum.

 To read the complete papers, go to dimensionsfoundation.org/research.

Science

The following statement from the National Science Education Standards, National Academy of Sciences, provides a nice summary of why the "minds-on-learning" that happens so well in Nature Explore Classrooms is of so much value to students.

"Learning science is something that students do, not something that is done to them. 'Hands-on' activities, while essential, are not enough. Students must have 'minds-on' experiences as well…Inquiry is central to science learning. When engaging in inquiry, students describe objects and events, ask questions, construct explanations, test those explanations against current scientific knowledge and communicate their ideas to others. They identify their assumptions, use critical and logical thinking, and consider alternative explanations. In this way, students actively develop their understanding of science by combining scientific knowledge with reasoning and thinking skills."

Social/Emotional

"Caring for simple things in nature – like caterpillars, flowers, and ladybugs – helps children develop a sense of themselves as nurturers and as people who care. This sense of self contributes to a peaceful way of living – with self, with others, and with the natural world." (Wilson, 2009)

Social and emotional development can flourish when children have frequent opportunities to experience care and empathy for the natural world as they work cooperatively with peers and adults. Technology and our fast-paced society have begun to limit children's opportunities to engage in the kinds of unstructured interactive play that has traditionally been a primary source of their social education. Nature-rich outdoor classrooms filled with loose parts and living things can provide a new kind of opportunity for children to develop their creativity, productivity and humanity.

The stories people sent us illustrated a wide range of ways that daily learning with nature can support children's social and emotional development. We have divided the stories into four broad categories of skills children were developing: A Positive Sense of Self; A Capacity for Caregiving; Feelings of Cooperation and Community; A Sense of Wonder.

A Positive Sense of Self

As Dr. Bruce Perry says in his book of the same title, all human beings are *Born for Love*. Infants come into this world hard-wired for interactions, seeking connections with those around them. Experiencing trusting relationships with primary caregivers is a crucial component of children's healthy emotional growth. Without this attachment, it is hard for children to develop a positive sense of themselves as individuals. Unfortunately, many parents and caregivers today report feeling high levels of stress, distraction, and isolation, which can all create barriers to healthy adult-child attachments. One way to overcome these challenges is by providing easily accessible and nurturing natural environments that reduce stress levels in both children and adults. Interactions with nature support feelings of calmness and tranquility, allowing people to truly be 'in the moment'. Studies show that as little as four minutes in a garden will start to reduce stress, improve mood, and steady the vital signs." (Easton, 2003)

The story below comes from a parent who has noticed the calming effect that regular time in nature has had on her children, and therefore on her ability to more deeply enjoy time together.

When You Slow Down
A parent's reflection

One of the things I have noticed with my youngest child is that when we are outside, he surprises me with the things that he notices. It's not just the obvious things like flowers, but he will look at the flowers long enough to find the insects on them. My children are teaching me to look longer or realize that there are so many dimensions to that flower. They are so peaceful when they are outside. They are comfortable and calm and I am too. Once you slow down enough to really engage with a child of that age, you begin to realize how enjoyable it is for you as an adult also.

Amy Schmaderer, Parent
Dimensions Early Education Programs, Lincoln, NE

Insights:

When children attend early childhood programs or elementary schools where time in nature-filled outdoor classrooms is a daily occurrence, adults often report noticing a positive change in children's behavior. When teachers and parents discuss the value of adding more nature connections to children's lives, both in and out of school time, families often begin to make nature outings a regular part of their weekly routines. As the story above notes, this time together can have a profoundly positive impact on parent-child relationships. In calm settings, parents are able to observe and celebrate their children's unique qualities, which, of course, helps children learn to celebrate and value themselves more fully.

Social/Emotional

The following story gives an example of the positive social and emotional benefits that time in nature-based outdoor classrooms can provide for all children including very young infants.

Social Babies
Sicily, 8 months and Aaron, 6 months

Aaron was sleeping on a blanket on the deck outdoors and Sicily was playing nearby on another blanket. When Aaron woke up he scooted toward Sicily. Face to face, they touched each other's hands, faces and jackets. After a few moments, Aaron moved so that he was able to touch the wood slats of the deck. Sicily watched him and then turned her body so that she was at the same corner of the blanket right next to Aaron. She reached her hand out to touch the deck, imitating what Aaron had done. They felt the slats with their fingertips, then their whole hands, sliding them along the wooden surface.

Anne Kärkkäinen, Infant Teacher
Child Educational Center, La Canada, CA

Insights:

These two infants were learning about themselves, each other, and the satisfying feel of a natural material (wood) as they explored the world at their fingertips. Opportunities to quietly explore unencumbered, to fully engage with others, and to enjoy calming sensory experiences with natural materials can often happen more easily in outdoor classrooms than in congested or noisier indoor spaces.

The story below is a reflection that comes from the director of a children's program in a domestic violence shelter. She talks about the positive changes she has observed since a Nature Explore Classroom was added to the shelter.

Good For Everyone
Infants, toddlers and preschool children

When we observed children in our newly added Nature Explore Classroom, we noticed that infants were more involved in touching, exploring, and using other sensory activities. They were more observant of their surroundings and stayed awake longer. Those who tended to cry frequently indoors were calmer when they were outdoors, and this calming effect lasted when they came back inside. Older infants were more alert and observant and spent more time investigating novel things together. They loved the sensory feel of the pine cones and were more alert and happy outdoors. The three-year-olds were able to sustain their involvement in activities for longer periods of time and interacted more with one another as they talked about the interesting things they found. They all enjoyed finding a caterpillar, observing its movements, and writing stories about it when they returned to the indoor classroom. On days when they were outdoors in the Nature Explore Classroom, the teacher noted that children were more relaxed and took great naps!

Joanne Osterland, Director
The Family Place Child Development Center
Dallas, TX

Insights:

Adults often use the word "calm" to describe nature-filled outdoor classrooms. Compare this to the often frenetic, hard-edged feeling of a traditional plastic and asphalt playground. Children who are surrounded by calmness and beauty are able to learn about more than the wonders of the world around them; they are also able to explore the wonders of their own inner worlds. This is quite a gift.

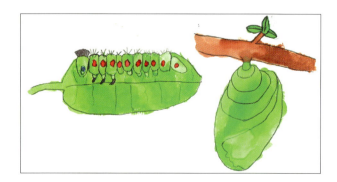

The following story provides a whimsical example of two children who feel free to express themselves.

Sometimes I Dream
Amanda and Hal, age 4

On a windy day running around our outdoor classroom with arms opened wide, eyes shut tight, twirling in the wind, Amanda said, "Sometimes I dream I am a butterfly and I'm flying." A short time later Hal came out and joined her, running around with his arms open wide, head up, saying, "It's raining popsicles. It's raining popsicles. It's raining strawberry popsicles."

Mona Abou Fakr, Preschool Teacher
Child Educational Center, La Canada, CA

Insights:

These children's poetic, creative language seems to reflect a joyful state of being and echo what American educator and poet E. Merrill Root meant when he said, "We need a renaissance of wonder. We need to renew in our hearts and in our souls the perennial sense that life is miracle and magic." (Root, 1974) Positive experiences create touchstones of strength in children that will serve them well throughout life.

In the photo above, a young girl who was exploring the Nature Explore Classroom at the Missouri Botanical Garden in St. Louis also pretended she was a butterfly.

Another way nature can help children strengthen a sense of self is by providing opportunities to do "real work." This positive type of activity is described below.

Pulling Broccoli
Preschool children

At the end of the growing season, each boy and girl was asked to help clear the garden by pulling out one of the old broccoli plants. The plants were rooted in tightly so some were very difficult to pull, especially for a four-year-old! After the children tried several times unsuccessfully to pull out the broccoli by themselves, a teacher began to help. What was great about this was that the teacher didn't do it for them. She still allowed the children to pull out the broccoli, just with her help. The photo of the teacher working with one little girl (left) shows the teamwork. The teacher pulled the child, who in turn pulled the broccoli plant! They laughed and laughed. Later they made the connection to the book, *The Giant Carrot*, having read it in class just the week before. In the book, each member of the family pulled on another until the giant carrot came out of the ground.

Darla Fontana, MS Ed., Director
WestLake Child Development Center, Houston, TX

Insights:

How wise the teacher was to work together with the children to support their efforts instead of doing the hard work for them. Experiences in the natural world are often most successful when caring adults skillfully support and scaffold children's learning. Without enough adult support (or with too much adult "help") children may become discouraged and give up. This can have a negative impact on how they feel about their capabilities. With just the right level of support, children will more easily develop positive feelings about themselves as competent and persistent people. And, as an added benefit, they may learn that hard work can be fun.

In the next story, a nature-filled setting encouraged elementary students with special needs to express individual feelings.

Charades in the Garden
Elementary school children

There's something about being outside that really stirs the creative juices. That is what I thought as I planned my social skills group. Typically, I bring students into my room and we play a variety of turn-taking games. But that day was one of those beautiful spring days and I was excited to go outside to our Nature Explore Classroom. Once outside, we headed toward the stage and played an inspired game of charades. Maybe it was the sun, or maybe it was the songbirds, but the kids really "got into it." One of the girls who typically has trouble accurately talking about past events, acted out several feelings. Another boy was able to pantomime a frustrating encounter he had with another peer earlier that day. In between skits, we watered vegetables in the garden and looked in on a mother nesting with her hatchlings. Only by assuring my students that we would return to the outdoor classroom soon were they willing to go back inside.

Noel Schecter, School Psychologist
Beard School, Chicago, IL

Insights:

Being surrounded by the beauty and gentleness of nature can encourage children to more openly and honestly explore their individuality. By providing continual opportunities to engage in real work, as well as to express individual thoughts and feelings, teachers can assist each child in developing a strong positive sense of self.

Social/Emotional

Read the account below of three middle schoolers who volunteered one summer to work in the Nature Explore Classroom they had attended as elementary students. Their self-confidence grew as they conceived of and successfully carried out a project to improve the classroom.

The Digging Area Project

Holly's Perspective: I served as coordinator for our middle school volunteers, Nic, Cady and Eve. I was amazed at how these students were able to carry out this project virtually on their own. They brainstormed, negotiated, and refined a design for the space, securing all the needed materials and tools. Then they tested it with younger children. There was much discussion and reflection after the construction phase of the space. It was a great experience for me to watch the kids in action.

Cady's Perspective: The question that started this project for me and the other volunteers was, "What can we do to help?" We decided to design a large Digging Area for children. We could see the one they had was too small. My first thought was that it would be pretty easy and quick to do this. We soon realized it was anything but that! It was not part of the volunteer job description, but we were ready for anything. About twenty hours, thirty ideas, and twenty sketches later, we made a decision about our plan. "This is a lot of thinking for one little patch of dirt," I said, and my quote became well known among us. Now, I've seen how our persistence and dedication paid off. The thing that amazed people most was that three seventh-graders created this idea, designed it and actually built it. I learned a lot about my work ethic, and myself and had fun. Most importantly, I had the joy and satisfaction of creating something that would make kids happy for decades to come.

Nic's Perspective: The Digging Area was made by three seventh-grade volunteers with clashing personalities (and I don't mean to boast) but we worked extremely well together. We went through the whole process of coming up with ideas for a design, making a floor plan, laying the brick and all the other little things involved with designing. But don't get me wrong, this was by far the highlight of my summer (even better than going to the Red Sox game at Fenway). Now, the finished product is a square brick path, which is painted like a jigsaw puzzle, that children can sit along as they dig in the dirt. It surprised me that three seventh-graders started and finished such a project without much help from anyone above age 12. Man, this will look good on my resume to become an architect!

Story coordinated by Holly Murdoch
School-age Teacher
Dimensions Summer Program, Lincoln, NE

Insights:

Students who believe in themselves as confident and competent people tend to take charge of their own learning and engage in academic tasks joyfully, not merely to please teachers. As this story illustrates, there is great value in involving older students as mentors who can support younger children's work in Nature Explore Classrooms.

Social/Emotional

A Capacity for Caregiving

"Deep bonds can form between children or a child and adult when they share experiences with nature. When children have daily opportunities to care for plants and trees, animals and insects, they practice nurturing behaviors that help them interact in kind and gentle ways with people as well." (Rosenow, 2008)

Frequent opportunities to experience caregiving for others and for nature help children define themselves as nurturers. These stories are great examples of what can happen in natural outdoor classrooms.

Don't Worry, Dallis Saved the Bird
Preschool children

It was early in the spring and we had just finished charting and counting all the birds that were returning from their winter migration. The children wanted to do something for all the birds. We had decided that filling our Nature Explore Classroom with bird feeders, bird baths, and various materials for nest building would be a wonderful welcome for our feathered friends. The children couldn't wait to refill the feeders and baths and see what goodies the birds decided to use for their nests. When I opened the door, they flooded outside in excitement. As I followed behind, I realized something was going on. All the children had gathered near the back of the yard. I walked over to see what had captivated their attention. As I neared, a bird lifted from the pack of children and zipped past my head. The crowd of children began to cheer and disperse. One little boy came up to me and said, "Don't worry Ms. Nancy, Dallis saved the bird. She's okay." With a little more investigating I learned that a small bird had gotten stuck in the chicken wire that lines our picket fence. Dallis was careful enough to free the little bird with no injury to either one.

Nancy Salerno, Preschool Director
Growing Minds Learning Center, Berkey, OH

Social/Emotional

Fall Fiesta
Levi, age 4

We have a school tree, named Fall Fiesta, planted and named several years ago by many children. It is a habit for children to check the tree regularly, often finding small ways to care for it, checking the moisture level in the soil, reminding others not to pull on the branches. Today, I watched as Levi spontaneously hugged the tree and I heard him say, "You are too young for me to climb right now, but someday you'll be big enough." This was eye-opening for me to see this tender, nurturing side displayed in Levi who clearly feels a connection to Fall Fiesta that has developed over time.

Katie Logan, Preschool Teacher
Dimensions Early Education Programs
Lincoln, NE

Insights:

A number of teachers have commented that when children are encouraged to name trees, caretaking feelings are strengthened.

Praying Mantis
Aden, age 5

Aden brought a praying mantis to school that had been caught in his back yard. He really wanted the praying mantis to live in the Nature Explore Classroom. To keep the praying mantis alive, he had been catching insects for it to eat. He said, "It's a bug, and it eats smaller bugs." To catch bugs to feed the praying mantis, Aden stated, "You have to run so fast so if you get 'em, you can catch 'em." Aden took the container with the praying mantis in it to the Garden Area. He carefully tipped the container sideways so the praying mantis could crawl onto the leaf of a plant. Aden asked children nearby not to touch it because he would feel sad if it got a broken wing.

Kathy Tichota, Preschool Teacher
Dimensions Early Education Programs Lincoln, NE

Insights:

Caring for living things such as plants, animals and insects allows children to connect with the tender, nurturing parts of themselves. Teachers who pay close attention to what children are doing and saying as they engage in caretaking behaviors can better support this important aspect of emotional development.

Social/Emotional

In the story below, a teacher rejoices as a child takes an important step forward in her social and emotional life.

A Beautiful Sight
Preschool children

Our outdoor space is a great setting for one young girl in our program to practice her caretaking skills. It's especially important because she doesn't have a mom at home. She'll gather bark for food and she'll gather greenery, sticks and twigs for silverware and dishes. She'll tell the children, "Now sit down. Open your mouth. Time to eat." And as she's pretending to feed them, it's a beautiful sight, because I know we're doing our job to help nurture her and help her grow.

LaTisha Whitfield, Preschool Teacher
Five Towns Early Learning Center
Inwood, New York

Insights:

Open-ended natural materials with nearly limitless possibilities for pretend play provide opportunities for children to act out a variety of roles. Teachers can learn much about what children are thinking by closely observing this type of play. In the story above, LaTisha was especially pleased to see her student taking on a mothering or caretaking role knowing that the little girl did not have a mother figure at home.

Social/Emotional

In the next story, an elementary school principal helped a struggling student re-define himself as a caretaker. The wise principal used real work in the outdoor classroom as a way to involve the student's family, as well.

Becoming a Helper
Jesus, Elementary school child

Jesus acted out in class all last year and the first quarter of this year was starting out the same. He was becoming a bully to other students and his teacher. When I met with his parents about his behavior, they were at a loss, too. They had been seeking outside resources, as well as working with our school resources. I had an idea and asked his dad if he would come work in our outdoor classroom with Jesus. His dad said he didn't have any time. When first quarter conferences came, I asked Jesus' classroom teacher to tell his father that I needed six holes dug and would he and Jesus come the next night at 6:00 p.m. The next night, at 6:00 sharp, Jesus found me in the library and said his dad, his godfather, and he were ready to dig holes. I really didn't think they would show up! I took them outside and showed them what I needed done. This was a really hard job because the dirt is clay. I came back forty-five minutes later and they were almost done. The dad and the godfather were praising Jesus so much because he did a great job. (This was all in Spanish). I gave them all Gomez Heritage Elementary School hats. They seemed to have had a great time. After that day, Jesus started being much more polite, saying, "Please," "Thank you," "Excuse me," and so on. He also started coming to adults to ask for help with students who were bothering him or messing around. The old Jesus would have joined in. I now have him help me in our Nature Explore Classroom once a week if we have a chance. I have since asked him to bring his dad in on another Saturday morning to put together some storage boxes. Again, they were happy to come. Jesus told his dad what to do in order to assemble the boxes correctly. Jesus loves going out to the outdoor classroom to help me, and his attitude and grades are going up.

John Campin, Principal
Gomez Heritage Elementary School, Omaha, NE

Insights:

This administrator was able to engage a struggling young student, and his family, in positive work that not only helped the school but also helped foster positive perspectives and relationships for everyone involved. Often, fathers report that parent volunteer activities seem more geared to women's interests than theirs. Opportunities for working in outdoor classrooms may engage some fathers (and perhaps some mothers) in ways that other activities might not.

Feelings of Cooperation and Community

"Efforts to foster positive social dispositions, tolerance for diversity, empathy, and cooperation all meet the criteria of helping children become model citizens – civic competence." (Epstein, 2009)

Natural outdoor spaces can certainly foster feelings of cooperation among children. It is unrealistic, though, to expect ever-idyllic and conflict-free play. In fact, that is not even a worthy goal. While reducing stress is positive, some conflict between children is inevitable, and can even be beneficial in small amounts so children have opportunities to develop coping skills and learn their own capabilities. Much like a muscle needs exertion to grow, children need doses of manageable stress and challenge to develop to their full potential. Nature-filled outdoor classrooms provide the time, space and calm setting that can support children in responding to experiences with an appropriate range of emotions. Teachers who encourage children to identify and label their feelings help lay the foundation for both a strong sense of self and the growth of empathy. As children grow in their independence, sense of self, and ability to communicate, they begin to become aware of others as separate beings with their own thoughts and emotions. This leads to greater forethought and less impulsivity. They become aware of the need for cooperation, and they start defining themselves as members of a wider community.

Read the next story to see how children were cooperating with friends while also exploring a social issue they noticed in their larger community.

Homeless Women
Rachel, Nancy, Lauren, Oliver, Randy and Brian, all age 4

Three girls were engaged in a discussion of what they wanted to do in the outdoor classroom. As they offered ideas, they seemed quite agreeable to each other's suggestions. When Rachel suggested building beds, Lauren replied, "Beds and no house?" Nancy then responded with a resounding, "Yeah!" They tossed questions and suggestions back and forth, each child building on the other's ideas. "Where will we live? We can be homeless. Homeless women." They began collecting boxes to use as beds. As they were building and talking, three boys came by and asked if this was a house. The girls quickly corrected them and explained they were making beds and that they were homeless women. Oliver asked to join the girls and they readily agreed, but told him that they were now "homeless people" because Oliver was not a woman. Two other boys indicated they also wanted to join in.

At this point, the three girls turned around and huddled together for discussion. They returned to tell the boys they could play, but the boys had to help make the beds. The six children continued to play, building beds and discussing how they would keep warm if they didn't have a house. After gathering sticks for a fire, they began to discuss how homeless people kept warm and made the observation that the homeless people they'd seen didn't have fireplaces to keep warm. Lauren speculated that they might use blankets, but Randy explained, "No, they don't have blankets. They just stay cold." Brian and Lauren remarked how sad that was.

Laura Campaña, Preschool Teacher
Child Educational Center, La Canada, CA

Insights:

As this teacher carefully documented words and actions, she gained a greater understanding of children's social skill development as well as a glimpse into how they were processing an important issue they had encountered in their wider community. The children's empathy for homeless people may impact many of their decisions later in life.

In the next story, an insightful teacher helps children work cooperatively on a "real work" task.

The Tree Team
Mackie, age 4 and Kiley, age 4

During our outdoor classroom time Mackie came up to me and said, "Mrs. Becerra, look, I found a little tree." I responded by saying, "Wow, that is really beautiful." I asked Mackie what his plan was for this tree. "I want to plant it," he responded. "What do you need?" I asked. "I need a bucket," he said. "What size?" I asked. "A big one," he replied. After gathering just the right tools I asked, "Is this going to be an all-by-yourself job or are you going to want to do teamwork with somebody?" He said he wanted to work with someone. I encouraged him to ask his peers to help him with his plan. He asked a few children and a little girl named Kiley said "I will help you." After they had planted the tree in a bucket using sand, I encouraged the negotiation of ideas between the two children about what to do with the planted tree. Kiley's idea was to decorate the tree with stickers. Mackie agreed, but the bird stickers wouldn't stick, so they had to problem-solve. They figured they could use a hole punch to make a hole on a piece of paper which they could adhere stickers to and then hook the paper onto the branches. The joy and satisfaction was evident on their faces as they worked, and through their excitement about the tree, other children were drawn in as well. Through this activity, Mackie and Kiley have forged a friendship. Almost every morning since that time, they meet each other at the sand area, and recreate the tree-planting experience. It's delightful to observe and listen to their conversations and see the friendship that has formed between these two children from different classes.

Blanca Becerra, Outdoor Classroom Coordinator and Teacher
Ascension Lutheran Early Childhood Center
Thousand Oaks, CA

Insights:

This story contains effective examples of how to "scaffold" children's learning in the outdoor classroom. This skillful teacher continued to ask questions that allowed Mackie to make his own decisions and think about how to accomplish his task. Her strategy of asking him if he wanted to work alone or with someone else respected his needs and abilities. It is important not to force children to work together before they have enough skills to tackle the hard work of negotiation and cooperation, but to continue to offer them the rewarding opportunity to "do teamwork."

Social/Emotional

The following story shows how one student's interests inspired an entire class.

Watching Chrysalises
Preschool children

I have a student named Noah. He loved to go and look for bugs in my Garden Area in the Nature Explore Classroom. One day he found some chrysalises hanging from a ledge. He was so excited, he got all the kids to come over and look at them. We talked a lot about how they looked, felt, and what would be coming out of them. Every day we would go outside and look at them to see if they had hatched. We were all thrilled to come outside one day and see them hatched and the butterflies still there. We watched them as they flew away. It was a great experience!

Michelle Avilla, Preschool Teacher
Kellom Elementary School, Omaha, NE

Insights:

Noah's close observation and excitement engaged other students in a study of a natural life cycle. Wise teachers realize that experiences such as this, led by student initiative, help children learn from each other.

Read below for another example of how natural settings can aide cooperative learning with older students.

Freedom and Cooperation
Elementary school children

The older children in the Learning Center (grades K-2) have engaged in quite a bit of role-playing activities. The freedom they have in the larger outdoor space has had a positive effect on their behavior. Often, if the children are not getting along indoors, the teacher may take them outside to the Nature Explore Classroom. It is evident that they become more cooperative with one another, more nurturing as they take care of the plants that they have planted, and happier as they dig in the sand. It's not something they often get a chance to do. They have also had discussions about taking care of the Earth, and the children are quick to take the time to pick up litter or other items that need to be discarded.

Joanne Osterland, Director
The Family Place Child Development Center
Dallas, TX

In the story below, a school community found a way to heal from a loss when their Nature Explore Classroom was dedicated as a memorial to a beloved teacher.

The Power of Nature to Heal a Community

Our outdoor classroom is a memorial to one of our teachers who died of a heart attack on the first day of school in 2009. It is a very sad story but much good has come out of it. Her husband and grown children have been healing from their loss by working in our outdoor classroom…building a stage, planting gardens, and more. They have been very dedicated to the project and we have named the classroom after her - Jan Gilbert Memorial Outdoor Classroom. It is a testament to the healing power of nature and the outdoors.

Stephanie A. Carlson-Pruch
Elementary Art Specialist
Gomez Heritage Elementary School
Omaha, NE

Social/Emotional

In the following story, a middle school teacher discusses how valuable it was for his students with special needs to take part in a community-wide gardening program at Fern Hollow Nature Center's Nature Explore Classroom.

Something Bigger Than Themselves

As a teacher, taking my students to Fern Hollow to start a garden was exactly what I needed to do. I was able to get to know my new students and reconnect with a few of my former students. I was introduced to parents, siblings and educators from other schools. Professionally, this project helped me grow as an educator. In addition, my classroom became a much larger place. Students were encouraged to generalize the appropriate behaviors learned in school. Academic, social and behavioral goals were addressed and reinforced quite easily in the garden setting. My autistic population thrived as the garden not only provided a social buffer, but lots of sensory stimulation as well. One of the greatest benefits was enrolling my students in an extracurricular activity. They appreciated being part of something greater than themselves. Their contributions were necessary for the success of the garden and group.

Jason Harrison, Learning Support Teacher
Quaker Valley Middle School
Sewickley, PA

Insights:

Feeling that one is a valued part of society is important to all of us, and especially beneficial for children with special needs. Planting and caring for a garden became one of the ways these students could define themselves as productive members of their community.

A Sense of Wonder

E.O. Wilson refers to the Earth as "the birthplace of our spirit" and suggests that "the more closely we identify ourselves with the rest of life, the more quickly we will be able to discover the sources of human sensibility." "Nature," he says, "settles peace on the soul." Wilson uses the term biophilia to refer to the "connections that human beings subconsciously seek with the rest of life." Without these connections, he says we cannot be whole. (Wilson, 1992)

Sometimes giving children a chance to experience nature means becoming comfortable with "messy" play. In the following story, a child development professor explains the joy children experience when they are allowed to explore freely in nature.

Mud, Mud and More Mud!
Preschool children

"Look at how gooey this is!" "I wonder if we can run, jump and splash big splashes?" The children enrolled in our center are provided experiences every day that allow nature to come alive in their hearts and minds. They love to explore the many facets of the elements, such as rain turning dirt into mud. Our Nature Explore Outdoor Learning Environment provides children numerous opportunities throughout the year to discover new words such as "mud" and "wet" and to use their senses (even tasting) to discover the elements in their natural state.

Kim Madsen
Child Development Professor
Chadron State College
Chadron, NE

Insights:

Not all families or educators are initially comfortable with children's "messy" play. Providing opportunities for staff and families to discuss the pros and cons of mud, for example, will help everyone think together about what experiences they want to provide for children. There are many ways to help children delight in nature's wonders, so it's important to find experiences that everyone can truly enjoy.

Social/Emotional

Children who spend daily time in nature often develop deep bonds with the living things they care for and nurture. A landscape architect wrote about children's reaction to the death of an "old friend."

Old Prickly

Preschool and elementary school children

One day recently, the inevitable happened. Old Prickly, a favorite evergreen, sweetly named by the children years ago, succumbed to old age. A storm took its toll and laid the tree on its side. The educators, ever so aware of the value the tree had for the children, observed their thoughts and feelings. At first, the children who had befriended the tree expressed sadness. It was not long though, before the children started making their way along the trunk from the base toward what was once the top. What had only been imagined from the ground was now observable from a very close viewpoint. Some collected cones. Others described the effort it took to "climb" the trunk, and the sensations of brushing against the branches and the stickiness of the sap. The roots and the size of the hole that was created by the upended tree fascinated others. One child made a song.

Jim Wike, Landscape Architect, Nature Explore
Excerpt from *Wonder, Exchange Magazine*
January/February 2011

Insights:

Because teachers involved children in the tree's removal and allowed parts of Old Prickly to remain in the outdoor classroom, they provided a respectful way to help children mourn their loss and learn about the cycles of life. Learning to come to terms with beginnings and endings in the life cycle is a lesson that nature gently teaches children who are allowed to form close bonds with the natural world.

Social/Emotional

The following story is another example of this kind of natural lesson.

The Cycle of Life
Preschool children

During the summer we had a whole program at our school based on nature, specifically insects. They were everywhere – spiders and beetles and earthworms – and the children were incredibly curious about them. They were thinking about these creatures as more than just "different from me." They were also thinking about them as valuable, as important enough to be taken care of. You know, we would see children take an ant from the classroom and gently take it outside. Respect for life, in any size that it comes in, is particularly for me a very important thing. Children also discovered very deep issues like death. That's something that we don't usually talk about. But outside it's there when somebody steps on an earthworm or a beetle. You know, they were discovering that their actions are deeply important. And, no teacher was telling them, "This is what happens if you do this." They were just naturally discovering things for themselves. And in the brain of each child, they were questioning, "Why doesn't it move? Is it hurt?" They were also personifying the insects: "The Mommy's crying. The Mommy's sad, and she's looking for her baby." All these things are very, very important and deep for a three-year-old to think about.

Bilma Krugman, Preschool Teacher
Five Towns Early Learning Center, Inwood, NY

Insights:

Because this teacher was paying close attention, she was able to see the deep learning taking place for children as they experienced nature's lessons. Now she will have the opportunity to help children discuss their thoughts and emotions. She can also help them articulate the lessons they are learning, such as the importance of handling living creatures with care and respect.

Social/Emotional

Following, is a story of how a wise teacher helped children develop a greater appreciation and feeling of responsibility for the wonders of nature.

The Nest Protectors
Owen, age 3, Sofia, Daniell, and Mareyi, age 4
Meg, Andrew, and Grant, age 5

A discovery was made up on our play structure in the outdoor classroom. A bird's nest was built in the crook of a beam on our structure within easy reach of children on the platform. This discovery sparked a big dilemma that the children had to problem-solve. The children were very worried about the placement that the momma bird chose. They wondered how to keep the nest safe. The group of children created a plan to protect the nest. "The nest is really not in a good place. I wonder what that silly momma bird was thinking?" said Meg. "We need to have nest protectors," said Grant. "And the protector needs a badge so everyone knows we are protecting the nest. It should be a star," said Andrew. The group decided to write a sign for the nest area to protect it. They included the words "no touching" and "only looking." The children took turns protecting the nest by standing watch and helping other friends to observe and not touch. They worried that the momma bird would not come back if they touched the nest. At first, the nest did not have an egg in it. We returned after a long weekend and there was a NEW discovery. The momma bird had laid an egg. "Now we really have to protect the nest," said Meg. The children started to talk about where the best place was for a bird to build a nest. They looked at books and closely checked for potential nesting sites all around the outdoor classroom. The children continued for two weeks to investigate birds and their habitats. The nest police guarded the nest the best they could, but one day the egg was taken out and ruined by a friend. We were able to have conversations about respect of nature and what happens when people don't protect animals, plants, and our Earth. The children wrote a note to the momma bird and shared what happened to the egg. The note also included a pledge from the children that they would try their best to protect all things in nature.

Jenny Leeper Miller, Master Teacher
Ruth Staples Child Development Laboratory
University of Nebraska-Lincoln

Insights:
Imagine how different this experience would have been for children if the teacher had simply removed the nest from the climbing structure. By allowing children to problem-solve and think carefully about their role as "protectors," she helped them take the first step on their journey toward environmental stewardship. Real, at-hand experiences like this are how young children learn to care for the Earth.

Social/Emotional

Me In The Picture

This is me in the picture. I said: "I am not going to touch it! It will really hurt!" And Mrs. Murdoc says: "It will not hurt." So I changed my mind. I want to take the plant home!

6-13-0

"Our lives are like streams. The currents of our experiences flow through time with periodic cycles of tranquility, disturbance, and integration. Our bodies are the banks of the stream, containing our life-energy..."

(Levine and Frederick, 1997)

Social/Emotional

The next story, sent in from an environmental educator, talks about the pure joy children experience when they are able to spend unhurried time in nature.

A Turtle and a Ladybug
Bridget, age 8 and Patrick, age 9

Bridget and Patrick are frequent visitors to Heritage Museums and Gardens, and with no exception they start at the Hidden Hollow Outdoor Discovery Center (a Certified Nature Explore Classroom). As campers in our summer program, they were exposed to daily adventures. But, the fun didn't end there. Every day after camp both children would ask mom to bring them back to Hidden Hollow for more exploration and play. The turtle and ladybug costumes became quick favorites of our two friends and both took their roles of forest creatures very seriously. Basically, from the moment they entered they would put on their costumes and then explore the area, pretending to be such creatures. Watching these two older siblings engage in simple creative play was refreshing and awe-inspiring. Their play would range from a run from one space to another, chasing one another, to quietly playing side-by-side making music with hardly a word between them. Even after hours of exploration, the two were never ready to leave, often asking mom for a few more moments. Both children explored and played in Hidden Hollow, as all visitors should, with pure comfort, inquiry and passion. Simply put, we could learn a lot by watching the way a turtle and ladybug enjoy their forest home.

Tobey Eugenio, Environmental Education Specialist
Hidden Hollow at Heritage Museums and Gardens
Sandwich, MA

Insights:

Well-designed outdoor classrooms offer endless, open-ended possibilities for exploration and discovery. Children who are engaged and active are far more likely to exhibit positive behaviors and build stronger social skills. As children share ideas, negotiate, make decisions, decide on tasks and roles, and problem-solve together, they develop a wide range of social and emotional skills. It is important for outdoor spaces to support a complete mix of activities and range of emotional needs throughout the day. Children will need both stimulation and solace outdoors depending on their learning style and mood. Having the chance to spend time in "hidey spots" or smaller spaces designed for quiet contemplation under a weeping willow tree or surrounded by tall prairie grasses can be both restorative and therapeutic.

Opportunities for this contemplative time can help address the well-documented pressures children face, such as those David Elkind wrote about in his book, *The Hurried Child*. A 2004 study published in the American Journal of Public Health found that symptoms of Attention Deficit Hyperactivity Disorder (ADHD) were significantly reduced in children as young as five when they engaged with nature. Jaak Panksepp from Washington State University has suggested that the increase in ADHD diagnoses in the U.S. may reflect that children no longer have adequate spaces in which to play each day. Adding nature-filled outdoor classrooms where children spend their days can ensure that every child has an "adequate" space to explore regularly.

These natural outdoor settings are especially important in places like domestic violence shelters where children have a whole host of emotions that they need to process. For this reason, the Mary Kay Foundation funded a series of Nature Explore Classrooms at domestic violence shelters throughout the United States. As one Mary Kay executive said during a dedication at one of the shelters, "Today is about good news…about the belief that trauma and tragedy do not replace play and purpose. It is about how our connection to nature can keep us connected to the best in ourselves and how this wonderful space is truly a healing garden for children and their families."

Social/Emotional

This final story speaks about one educator's realization of what time in her outdoor classroom can mean to her students on an emotional level.

A Sacred Space
Elementary children

Every time I take my students to our outdoor classroom it is a rich experience unlike any other during the school day. We exit the school building and breathe in the fresh air. There is a sense of freedom that rushes through us. The moment we enter the O.C., as we endearingly call it, we all stop and gasp, taking in a deep breath, as if for the first time. It is always breathtakingly beautiful to enter the nature space, as if we have entered a sacred space. It is!

I have always loved nature. When I was a child, I played outside every chance I got. As an adult, I hike, swim, camp, and take walks in nature for physical, emotional, and spiritual benefits. As an educator, I feel that nature provides unique and even rare opportunities for learning. I am very structured in the indoor classroom and keep noise and movement to a minimum, unless directly needed for learning. As a result, it has been a challenge for me in the O.C. to let my students explore freely, moving throughout the space and interacting with nature at any sound level they feel necessary. I have struggled in "letting go" and am overcoming this resistance slowly. To feed my need for more structured curriculum, I present an idea to my students upon entering the O.C. Sometimes the idea is an invitation to record sensory experiences, to build, make and draw, or to work in groups on a theme-based idea.

As I observe my students in the O.C., I remember how boundless I felt and still feel in nature. I want them to experience that as purely and as unrestricted as possible. After attending Nature Explore educator workshops, I am up for the challenge!

Stephanie Carlson-Pruch
Elementary Art Specialist
Gomez Heritage Elementary School
Omaha, NE

Insights:

As this educator readily admits, learning to "let go" of a need for control can be a challenge when supporting children in an outdoor classroom. The older the student, the more appropriate it becomes for teachers to provide "curriculum" ideas for using the space. The younger the child, the more the ideas for how to use the space should flow from the child's own intrinsic motivation. With younger students, the teacher's challenge is to carefully observe, document and scaffold children's learning. With older students the challenge is to allow enough freedom for children to explore curriculum topics in a way that will meet individual interests and help foster social and emotional development. Natural outdoor spaces provide a chance for children to learn different lessons that the indoor classroom cannot provide. Teachers may need to learn to interact with students in new ways in the outdoor classroom and to pay attention to different kinds of skills to support – such as social and emotional skills. Exploring the wonders of nature can help all of us connect more fully with the grandness of the world community we share and with the internal world that is uniquely ours.

From Dimensions Foundation Research

Excerpts from *Young children develop foundational skills through child-initiated experiences in a Nature Explore Classroom: A single case study in La Canada, California* by Ellen Veselack, Lisa Cain-Chang and Dana L. Miller, 2011.

Identifying with nature and nurturing living things are every day occurrences in Nature Explore Classrooms. In the following examples, children have internalized the natural rhythms of life.

- In a Nature Note, when children came outside on a very windy day, Amanda observed the trees, drew on previous knowledge, and cautioned the others: "Some branches, if they're not steady, they will break.

- In another Nature Note, three-year-old Allen was collecting food for his worm when a peer approached to help, and added rocks and sand to the container. Allen observed his friend's contribution and shared that he was "not gonna take the sand because worms don't eat sand."

Excerpts from *This never would have happened indoors: Supporting preschool-age children's learning in a Nature Explore classroom in Minnesota* by Vicki Bohling, Cindy Saarela, and Dana L. Miller, 2011.

- The majority of play observed in the Nature Explore Classroom was initiated by the children. Only 18% of the Nature Notes represented adult-directed activities. Many observations made no mention of the teacher or noted the teacher's presence in a very peripheral manner. It is evident that complex, adult-directed activities are not required to produce the type of rich skill development observed in our data. For young children, the emphasis of experience over information is important. Authentic learning requires access to real objects and open-ended materials that can be freely manipulated. Both are in abundant supply in a Nature Explore Classroom.

- As we undertook this study the experience of children with special needs was of particular interest since there is limited information regarding this population in outdoor settings. In focus group interviews teachers reported that children with sensory integration issues or who struggled to stay on task indoors were often calmer and more focused outside.

Excerpts from *The seeds of learning: Young children develop important skills through their gardening activities at a Midwestern Early Education Program* by Dana L. Miller, Ph.D. in Applied Environmental Education and Communication, 6:49-66, 2007. (Note: This publication is not available on the Dimensions Web site.)

- Experiential learning gives them (children) opportunities to "feel" more connected to nature and to process their emotions. Often, through experience and teacher support, children learn to take risks, develop self-confidence, and gain mastery over their fears. (p. 59-60)

- With teacher support the outdoors also becomes a safe place to express positive emotions and learn to process and manage negative emotions. Children learn courage and confidence and how to successfully interact with others as they explore the wonders of nature together. (p. 64)

Access to three-dimensional materials provides opportunities for children to act out fearful situations and helps children feel a sense of mastery over their fears. To read more about this, go to: *Working Hypothesis* at www.natureexplore.org/research.

To read the complete papers go to dimensionsfoundation.org/research.

Mathematics

"Why can't we help parents to see their children as delightful little scientists, architects, explorers, acrobats, and scholars who use all their senses, their whole bodies, and their own behavior as the tools for astonishingly thorough, albeit messy, investigations in the world of people and things?" (Greenman, 1989)

"Experiences and intuitive ideas become truly mathematical as the children reflect on them, represent them in various ways, and connect them to other ideas." (Excerpt from Early Childhood Mathematics: Promoting Good Beginnings: A joint position statement of the National Association for the Education of Young Children and the National Council of Teachers of Mathematics, 2010)

Nature provides a multitude of interesting materials that inspire budding mathematicians to measure, count, sort, and fit together.

Natural outdoor classrooms provide engaging opportunities for children to develop valuable mathematical concepts through frequent hands-on investigations. The variety and quantity of open-ended loose parts encourage children to find and create patterns, explore the idea of "number," and "mathematize" their thinking. The term "mathematize" comes from the position statement referenced above, which encourages adults to think more intentionally about appropriate early mathematical experiences. When children in Nature Explore Classrooms are supported by engaged and informed adults, "mathematized" thinking can flourish from the earliest months of life through the elementary school years.

Many of the stories sent to us from Certified Nature Explore Classrooms referenced the mathematical skills children were demonstrating (such as counting, estimating, and measuring). While these skills are certainly important, it's also helpful for adults to realize how essential it is for children to develop intuitive and authentic understandings of mathematical processes. These more complex ways of thinking include: using logical reasoning to solve problems; communicating mathematical ideas; and connecting mathematical concepts to everyday life. In this chapter's stories you will see real-life examples of children using mathematical processes in their play. At times the stories seem deceptively simple, but if you look deeply you'll see that valuable, foundational mathematical thinking is developing.

Mathematics

The three stories below illustrate how open-ended natural materials support very young children's growing mathematical understandings.

The Value of Rocks
Toddler children

We encourage all of our toddlers to build with, carry, sort, and move the rocks in our Garden Area. We know that this feels like real work to them, which it is because these kinds of experiences are actually helping the toddlers to internalize understandings of classification, pattern, and number concepts.

Elena Otto, Assistant Director
Kids and Company Childcare at
Lakeshore Learning Materials, Carson, CA

Insights:

By documenting seemingly simple experiences with rocks, teachers came to understand the important math concepts being developed, even though children did not yet have the vocabulary to describe their thinking.

As two year-old Rex played with rocks and stones in the garden, the varied weight, shape, color, and texture of these natural objects provided him with complex mathematical learning opportunities and helped him feel connected to the world around him.

Counting Beans
Danny, age 26 months

Danny appeared curious about what was inside the bean he had picked from our garden. He wanted to open it, but after trying for several minutes on his own, he asked me for help. Once I got it started for him, he opened it all the way and laid the two halves of the bean pod on top of our wooden stage. He looked at the seeds for quite awhile, then took the seeds from one side of the pod and put them back into the other side, counting as he went: "one, two, three…"

Katie Dietz, Toddler Teacher
Dimensions Early Education Programs, Lincoln, NE

Insights:

In this instance, Danny is already using his mathematical thinking as part of his play. Nature's loose parts (the beans) are so significant in this story because of Danny's deep interest in a material he has grown and then picked himself. This is a different experience than he would have had indoors with manufactured materials that are not meant to be taken apart.

Counting Peas

Josie, age 34 months, Everett, age 33 months, Rowan, age 32 months

For several minutes Josie and Everett picked and opened pea pods, then laid them out on a large stump. Next, Josie took several of the peas, laid them on the wood slats on the ground nearby where she sat, and peeled the skin off each one. Still standing, Everett counted the peas as he laid them on the stump. "1, 2, 3, 4, 5, 6, 7, 8, 9, 10, 11, 15, 17, 18, 19, 20. They are all mine!" he said. Rowan watched Everett then asked, "Do you want some more?" Everett said, "Yes," so Rowan ran over to the garden to look for more.

Kaysha Brady, Toddler Teacher
Dimensions Early Education Programs, Lincoln, NE

Insights:

Notice that because of the properties of the peas, the children's thinking quickly becomes mathematical. They modeled a variety of mathematical language for each other (such as counting and using the word "more").

Now read how preschool-age children communicated about their math experiences.

Two Sticks
Eli, age 4

Eli walked up to me in the Nature Explore Classroom and said, "I found two sticks." He carried a thick stick in each hand. One measured about two and one-half feet and the other about two feet. Eli then told me, "I measured them." Holding out the longer stick he said, "This one is taller." Then holding out the shorter stick, Eli accurately said, "This one was a little bit shorter." He seemed to be measuring them by comparing them to his own height. Later, we recalled children's activities as a group and I asked Eli to tell his friends about his sticks. He accurately showed them with his hands (in relationship to the ground) how tall each stick was.

Kathy Tichota, Preschool Teacher
Dimensions Early Education Programs, Lincoln, NE

Leaves
Derek, age 5

I saw Derek playing with a pile of leaves and asked him about them. He explained that he had collected them from under a tree nearby. I asked about his plan for the leaves and he told me they were just for looking at, but then described their size: "There are some big ones – like this one. It's bigger than those, it is the biggest." Next he pointed to others, noting their relative size and moving them into position from smallest to largest. When I asked him to tell me about what he had done, he counted 27 leaves in a line. I told him that I noticed he had not only counted 27 leaves, but also pointed out to him that he had lined them up in order by their size.

Holly Murdoch, Preschool Teacher
Dimensions Early Education Programs, Lincoln, NE

Insights:

The child-initiated tasks described in the stories above were "mathemitized" by the scaffolding of teachers who helped shape children's experiences and reinforce their thinking. The complexity of what nature provided, with all the variables, required Derek especially to do some deep thinking about his yellow leaves. His teacher, through her presence during the process, was able to document (and celebrate for Derek) much more than just rote counting, but also his ability to seriate (arrange in order by size).

In the next few stories, children enjoyed building structures with loose parts on a scale large enough for them to be in and on. Here, mathematical learning was taking place alongside experiences with creative dramatics and literacy.

From Rocks to Roads
Preschool and kindergarten children

Our Nature Exploration Area provided the perfect setting for an imaginary town. Children built the town's houses and roads one afternoon using rocks, poles, hay bales, and sand. A variety of tools, including galvanized buckets, helped with the hauling of smaller rocks. The spontaneous team efforts included creating sturdy houses from long six-foot wooden poles chosen from a pile with a variety of sizes. "These are soooo heavy! It'll take three of us to drag this log to make our fort!" said Jack to Eric. At the same time and place, another group was working with different intentions: "This road is for the wedding at the church," said Tai, as she added more rocks, then walked arm-in-arm with Kathryn down the "bride's path." The wonderful thing in both these projects was that the imagination came from the children first. These materials are always available and provide endless opportunities for creative exploration, storytelling, and mathematical learning. I was able to weave in literacy and reinforce their creativity by reading the book *Roxaboxen* by Alice McLerran. The book celebrates the imagination of children who, no matter the time or place, can create whole worlds out of what they find around them.

Mary Skow, Head of School
St. Thomas Early Learning Center
College Station, TX

Insights:

There is certainly whole-child learning happening in this story, and math processes are embedded throughout. Children first sorted and classified the materials available to them by identifying and then comparing the characteristics of each. (They also used a visual-spatial skill to sort through their "mental library" of images of various kinds of structures they had seen. They could then "retrieve" the images they wanted to use to design and build their town. Creating the structures involved using several math skills to solve construction problems, including figuring out whole-to-part and scale relationships, and estimating the size of the town's perimeter. These kinds of real-life experiences allow children to deeply understand mathematical concepts before they are able to talk about them. At a later time in their lives, they will learn the more sophisticated vocabulary words (such as "perimeter") that they can attach to the concepts they already understand.

Mathematics

In this teeter-totter story, children used mathematical thinking to find the correct lengths of logs and the appropriate sizes of rocks with which to create.

The Teeter-Totter
George and Xavier, age 4

George and Xavier learned about cooperation, balance, and coordination as they played on a natural teeter-totter they made in the Messy Materials Area. Throughout the process of creating this structure, children also measured the different materials, made a poster noting their length, and learned the word "circumference."

Elena Otto, Assistant Director
Kids and Company Childcare at
Lakeshore Learning Materials, Carson, CA

Insights:

Teachers provided the time needed to create this elaborate structure, and they helped scaffold children's mathematical learning throughout the experience. Notice all of the thinking children had to use to determine where to place the fulcrum of the log so it would balance and function as a teeter-totter. All this math learning took place while the children were also doing the physical labor of lifting and moving the logs, and using the social skills needed to work together successfully. The teacher extended the students' thinking by providing paper and markers and helping them make charts of the logs' lengths and weights.

The story below illustrates how elementary students used mathematical thinking (and other skills) during a large construction project.

Sand Rivers
Elementary school students

Impressed by the large-scale project work of author and artist Andy Goldsworthy, our class worked collaboratively to create a large "sand river." First, children looked at pictures of similar works from Goldsworthy and then discussed the tools they would need for such a big job. After gathering everything from the outdoor classroom's storage area, the children eagerly got to work digging. Once the installation was completed, the students were observed walking along the river path and even measuring it with their bodies. This activity fostered the children's visual/spatial and kinesthetic learning by encouraging them to look at the world from different perspectives, and it strengthened their mathematical thinking as they explored size relationships.

Caitlin Bouse, Teacher
Elmhurst Academy of Early Learning, Elmhurst, IL

Insights: Children needed something readily available, flexible, and meaningful with which to measure the scale of their project. Their bodies turned out to be just the right tool for this kind of measurement!

Mathematics

On a family outing at Arbor Day Farm's Nature Explore Classroom, this child used mathematical skills to determine which logs would be long enough to create the perimeter of her hideout.

Read below for another example of how children's mathematical thinking was supported as children built with nature's "loose parts." Much like in the previous story, children had to figure out how big a perimeter to create in order to make their structure large enough for them to fit in. The teacher who sent this story told us the children carefully selected logs with uniform lengths, then created right angles as they built their enclosure.

Bear Den
Preschool children

While playing with logs, several children decided to build a home for bears. They talked about where bears live and decided to make a "den" using the logs. They carried logs over and placed them across some stumps, creating a rectangle. Several children crawled under the logs, then noticed: "We need more." (The structure was not yet big enough to allow enough children to fit inside.) As they moved the five-foot logs around, I saw the children help each other and work as a team, especially to move the heavier logs. The children joyfully sang as they moved and stacked the logs. After getting all the logs stacked, the children took turns crawling in the "den," pretending to be bears. When we went back into the indoor classroom, we added bear books to the Book Area.

Paula Southworth, Teacher
Webster County Early Learning Center
Blue Hill, NE

Insights:

Building on a large scale and math seem to go together. Paula Southworth also told us another story about the mathematical thinking and communication children used on another day. Using large fabric, they built a tent around an existing teepee frame. Children talked about which colored fabric pieces to use on top and which on the bottom, based on the sizes of the pieces. The frame was tall, so children needed to find out who among them was tallest and could reach the top to put the fabric on. They needed to estimate and measure many things to successfully complete both the bear den and the teepee project, both of which were much too large to be done in the indoor classroom.

Mathematics

Consider all the mathematical terms and classification skills the girls in the following story are using, as well as how their teachers have taught them to independently solve problems.

Healthy Dog Salad
Preschool children

When our teachers first explored the idea of what we wanted for children in our outdoor classroom we agreed that we wanted them to be able to experience the joy of picking flowers. So to provide this opportunity, we planted a vine that is covered with plenty of "pickable" flowers. We also take advantage of every chance to engage children in conversation about which flowers to pick, which ones to just look at and the ecological reasons and considerations for this thinking. One day we observed as two girls picked greenery to make "a healthy salad for the dogs to eat to get better in the dog hospital." As we listened to these four-year-olds making their salad, we heard the following conversation:

"I can pick just one of these white flowers because there are quite a few of them but not too many."

"We can't pick the yellow ones because they grow from bulbs and only have one."

"If we pick that, then nobody else can see it."

"Yes, and it will die sooner."

"If we need a lot we can pick the mint because it grows a lot."

It was very validating to hear how these children had internalized and learned from our conversations and how they had become proficient in expressing those ideas to each other.

Sue Davis, Teacher and Judy Hightower, Director
Westminster Presbyterian Church Preschool, Westlake Village, CA

Insights:

Obviously this is a story about more than children's growing mathematical thinking. Children also were developing a sense of themselves as caretakers and nurturers as they assessed which flowers could be picked and which could not. Isn't it nice to see how two valuable skills were being supported simultaneously through a very motivating nature-based experience?

In the following story, some mathematical "wheeling and dealing" took place.

Selling Gourds
Kindergarten children

In the fall, kindergarteners were using many areas of the outdoor classroom in unstructured exploration when I heard students "selling" gourds and mini-pumpkins. The sellers had little wheelbarrows full and they set up a roadside shop and started calling out to the buyers. Soon students were flocking to the "store" to buy, and imaginary money came out of pockets. There was even haggling over prices, with certain items going for a premium based on size, shape, color, and weight of the gourds. One vender confided in me that he bought the gourd for fifty cents but was selling it for a dollar! The secret markups of the selling group were the source of much delight among them. There were comparisons and decisions to make, and the buyers were delighted with their purchases.

The merchandise was traded all over the outdoor classroom that day.

Julia Gilreath, Elementary Art Specialist
Gomez Heritage Elementary School, Omaha, NE

Insights:

Children engage in grocery store play both indoors and out. This story seemed special to us because the variety of materials outdoors seemed to spur more excited dramatic play, creative pricing and flexible thinking than is often seen indoors. Notice the enthusiasm and excitement for play that has math integrated throughout.

Mathematics

The family in the following story adopted a garden plot at their children's school. Caring for the garden all summer long became a labor of love for them. Read below for accounts written from both a daughter's and a father's perspectives. Watch especially for the size comparisons and other mathematical thinking that Mary Ellen includes in her story. Father Tim discusses how nature became an important part of this family's culture.

A Garden within a Garden
Mary Ellen Mack, age 10

My sister and I have a garden that only measures 3 feet by 4 feet. It is located in the middle of a garden 100 times its size, but for a season it was the center stage for my family. Last spring my sister and I came with our shovels to dig out the clay. We worked with peat moss and fertilizer before we planted a dozen sunflowers that all started from seeds. Over the summer the sunflowers kept growing. By the end of June the sunflowers were taller than my dad who is 6 feet tall. On the beautiful Sundays of July and August we would always check on the garden. My sister and I had a lovely experience picking and eating the tomatoes. But that summer the sunflowers stole the spotlight of the Beard School Garden. The sunflowers were just perfect. When it was autumn we dug a little hole by the sun flowers and we found a boat-load of worms. So we knew that was how the sunflowers grew so big. There was a little miracle in the Beard School Garden in the spring and summer of 2010.

Mary Ellen Mack, Sister of a student at Beard School, Chicago, IL

Emily and Mary Ellen Mack's Garden
Tim Mack, Father

It all started with a simple note sent home from school last spring requesting help working in the school garden. For me it was easy to lend a hand because time in the garden isn't work at all. I went to the garden with my two girls, first-grader Emily who attends the Beard School and her older sister Mary Ellen. Both of my girls pitched right in at our new adopted garden. We carved ourselves out a new little plot with an old picket fence from home and we planted a dozen sunflower seedlings. Over the summer we watched them grow up to twelve feet high. But I have a secret to tell. It is not only the plants that grew all summer in that garden. My wife, May, who was often reluctant to work in our yard at home, grew to love our time in the school garden. During the summer the four of us would walk to the garden often more than once a day. We figuratively got to enjoy the fruits of our labor as we watched the garden grow but we also literally enjoyed the fruits. I don't know if we brought home more tomatoes or ate more there!

Insights:

Many teachers and parents have reported siblings enjoying time together in the outdoors with less conflict than often happens indoors. Parents of children with special needs have shared stories relating new strengths emerging in those children that were made visible to their brothers and sisters when working together in nature.

From Dimensions Foundation Research

Excerpts from *More than play: Children learn important skills through visual-spatial work* by Dr. Dana L. Miller, 2004.

- Through visual-spatial work, young children are also introduced to basic math concepts, such as base, height, width, length, and size. They develop early math skills including sorting objects by shape, color and size; counting; recognizing groups and patterns; sequencing; and recognizing numbers. Young children are even being introduced to fractions as they work with blocks.

Excerpts from *The seeds of learning: Young children develop important skills through their gardening activities at a Midwestern Early Education Program* by Dana L. Miller, Ph.D. in Applied Environmental Education and Communication, 6:49-66, 2007. (Note: This publication is not available on the Dimensions Web site.)

- Through children's work in the garden/greenhouse they are communicating what they know about their world. They may not be able to verbalize their knowledge, but if we closely observe them, they will show us. Often that knowledge is much more sophisticated than we realize.

Excerpts from *This never would have happened indoors: Supporting preschool-age children's learning in a Nature Explore classroom in Minnesota* by Vicki Bohling, Cindy Saarela, and Dana L. Miller, 2011.

- Children demonstrated their ability to identify patterns by noting pumpkins at school, pumpkins at the pumpkin patch, and pumpkins at home. They also discovered a pattern between types of seeds – pumpkin seeds and corn seeds. Children experienced quantity in a tactile way as they selected seeds with their fingers for planting. They used descriptive vocabulary to articulate size differentiation – "small, big, middle size."

Excerpts from *Young children develop foundational skills through child-initiated experiences in a Nature Explore Classroom: A single case study in La Canada*, California by Ellen M. Veselack, Lisa Cain-Chang, and Dana L. Miller, 2011.

- Interacting with natural materials, peers, and teachers in the Nature Explore Classroom provided children with many opportunities to develop early math skills... Children explored patterns, the attributes of objects, and shapes. They encountered opportunities to estimate, measure and count. Children explored concepts of quantity and used quantity vocabulary, explored size... demonstrated one-to-one correspondence, and counted frequently. These early math experiences were especially meaningful for children because they initiated them. They engaged in math that was part of the context of the activities they chose to initiate.

- As young children engaged in mostly child-initiated activities in the Nature Explore Classroom they used math in multiple ways; to explain themselves to others, to recount recent events and to help solve their problems. They physically experienced many mathematical concepts because of the nature of the space, the configuration of the areas, and the specific materials available. Those concepts included volume, area, perimeter, diameter, circumference, length, height, width, size, and geometric shapes. They observed whole-part relationships firsthand. They used math concepts naturally, in the context of their play, which allowed them to begin to understand the function of mathematical concepts in ways that were meaningful to them.

 To read the complete papers, go to dimensionsfoundation.org/research.

Body Competence

"I don't know why the idea of mind and body as separate entities took hold or why it's lasted as long as it has. But more and more, we have evidence that this is a false notion. And while I'm delighted with all the research pointing to the body's role in cognitive development and learning, as a children's physical activity specialist, I feel quite strongly that the body matters, too – that physical development and physical fitness deserve equal respect and attention!" (Pica, 2010)

Active running, climbing, and games are often associated with recess in school and backyard play at home. These experiences are important to physical health, but are only a part of overall physical development. In Nature Explore classrooms, with their complete mix of activities, children have opportunities for comprehensive physical development. Chances for multi-sensory learning, appropriate risk-taking through active play, real work, healthy eating, and self-calming activities are all important for optimal physical development. This chapter has stories grouped together in those categories to illustrate the many ways that nature contributes to children's development of body competence skills.

In their book *Thinking Goes to School: Piaget's Theory in Practice*, Hans Furth and Harry Wachs say:

"The importance of movement thinking should not be underestimated. If the six-year-old child does not have fundamental control over both general and discriminative movements, he will find it difficult, if not impossible, to move his eyes across the page, look up and down from the chalkboard to his paper, hold a pencil, or compete in play with his peers…If bodily movement is well under control, children can expend minimum energy on the physical mechanics of the task and maximum energy on the thinking related solution."

Multi-Sensory Learning

One outcome of children's disconnection from nature is a lack of sensory stimulation. Increased time in sterile indoor environments, use of manufactured plastic toys, and earlier and prolonged use of electronics all decrease opportunities for children to use all of their senses. This is especially concerning since the window of opportunity to best develop the senses of sight, touch, smell, taste, and hearing is during the preschool years. Despite children's physical capability to perceive sensory stimulation well during this time, practice processing that sensory information is vital for healthy brain and central nervous system development. Many educators are wondering if the growing rise in children identified with behavioral problems and sensory-processing disorders is related to a lack of consistent time outdoors. The stories in this section, representing each of the five senses, are rich examples of how children's experiences outdoors support their sensory learning.

Outdoor sensory experiences are extremely beneficial for infants and toddlers because it is mainly through their senses that they are collecting information and learning to understand the world around them. This developmental window of opportunity is unfortunately often the time when many educators and parents seem most hesitant to take young children outdoors.

The story below provides a great example of how Nature Explore Classrooms can support sensory exploration.

Exploring the Space
Lulu, age 10 months

Lulu sat on some blankets and pillows, chewing on a toy and eyeing the yard. She moved over to the leg of the shade canopy and pulled herself to a standing position. She dropped down and crawled across the grass to the chain-link fence. Once again, she pulled herself to a standing position and stepped up onto the three inch cement curb at the base of the fence. She dropped down and sat in a pile of small leaves. She swished her hands through the pile on either side of her a few times, then picked up leaves and squeezed them in her hands, listening to the crunching sounds they made. She dropped them from her hands and watched them fall to the ground. She crawled over to the sand box and leaned over the edge with one hand in the sand. After exploring the sand for several minutes, she moved over to the tree and stood, leaning her hands on the tree. She touched the tree with the palms of her hand and her fingers. She tasted the tree, sticking her tongue out and delicately licking the bark. She looked at the bark intently before looking up and discovering another child nearby.

Teresa Roldan, Teacher
Child Educational Center, La Canada, CA

Insights:

Exploration was Lulu's agenda. Her teacher was supporting it by staying out of the way, while still intently documenting learning and keeping a watchful eye on safety. If her teacher had chosen to interact with Lulu, the focus might have shifted from a materials exploration to a social interaction. Lulu may have missed the sound of the crunching leaves or the taste of the tree! The natural space provided a great "learning lab" where she could experiment with her own physical capabilities while also gaining new information about the wonders of the natural world. Free exploration for young children like Lulu only happens in natural settings when care providers feel they can adequately supervise and monitor the risks of loose parts within reach. This is why intentional space design and ongoing safety discussions are both vital for adults working with infants and toddlers.

Compare the sensory exploration of a three-year-old in the story below, to younger Lulu's experiences.

My Hands in the Sand
Talen, age 3

While I was visiting the outdoor classroom at Jewel's Learning Center, several boys chose to play in the Sand Area with some new tools. My attention was captured by Talen. He seemed to be watching several of the boys who were a year or so older than he. After Talen followed the older boy's lead by taking off his shoes and socks and lining them up with everyone else's, he walked into the sand box and sat right in the middle of about six other children. I noticed that Talen was very quiet as he scooped sand with a shovel and slowly poured it into his bucket. He repeated this same action over and over again. Sometimes he grabbed a fist-full of sand and watched it slide through his fingers. Sometimes he took the tiniest pinch of sand and rubbed it between his thumb and finger as he dropped it into his bucket. Once in awhile Talen would wiggle his toes down into the sand and lift his feet into the air, watching the sand fall as the wind blew it away or as it fell back to the ground. Even an hour later, Talen was completely immersed in this experience, never seeming to be distracted by the very active play and conversations that surrounded him. As Talen got up to leave the Sand Area, I saw him take a few steps and then slowly and deliberately tap the sand very gently with the tips of his toes, take a few more hopping steps and do it again, and then again, always watching the sand as he touched it with his feet.

Tina Reeble, Nature Explore Education Specialist Visiting Jewel's Learning Center, Houston, TX

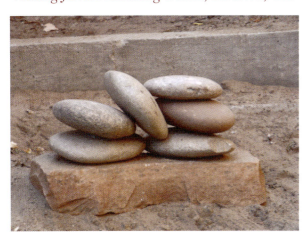

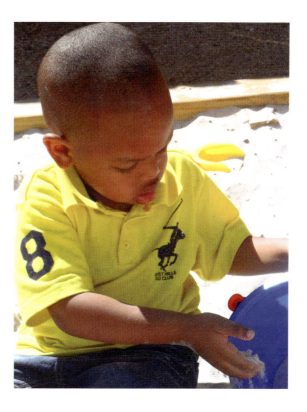

Insights provided by Tina Reeble:

I can't say what Talen was thinking about during that hour of play, but I believe it must have been very meaningful for him because of his intense focus. What I saw was a child thinking about the way things feel and move. I'm not sure that Talen would even be able to describe his experience with words; it is something that right now his body understands through feeling. With regular experiences over time, this "body knowledge" will become the intuitive foundation that supports Talen's understanding of many science, literacy, and math concepts. I hope we early educators make a point to allow children these longs periods of pure physical exploration.

Body Competence

As the stories below illustrate, changing weather conditions in outdoor classrooms provide "new curriculum."

New Experiences in Snow
Toddler children

Snow and winter weather changed the outside experiences for the children with new scenery and terrain. The Toddlers have been able to observe how the snow feels, what it looks like and sometimes how it tastes! Cody made a snow angel while we were outside and was pleased with the design that he made by moving his whole body in the icy snow. Danny sat on the snow and soon realized how cold and wet it felt on his pants. The children love being outside in any weather, and for many of the children at this age, snow is a new experience in temperature, texture, and mobility.

Kaysha Brady, Toddler Teacher
Dimensions Early Education Programs,
Lincoln, NE

Insights:

This wise teacher knows that snow is not a reason for keeping children indoors. There is much learning waiting to happen through explorations of all kinds of weather conditions. The key to making this work is good communication with parents and some pre-planning for how to deal with clothing issues. Many teachers keep stashes of inexpensive boots and mittens on hand for all children so that a quick trip into interesting weather is always an option. Honest staff discussions about how to deal with extremes in cold and hot temperatures are necessary so that children are always kept safe. Families need to be involved and informed, as well, so everyone feels comfortable with the outdoor policies of the organization.

Gooey, Sticky Sand
Tristan, age 3

On a chilly November morning in the Sand Area I sketched and took notes on what children were working on. Tristan explained to the friend next to him, "We need more of the sticky sand." The boys had found a pot of sand that was wet from rain. The wet sand stuck more easily to the pumpkin that they were trying to cover up. "We need the gooey sand," they repeated.

Kris Van Laningham, Preschool Teacher
Dimensions Early Education Programs, Lincoln, NE

Insights:

In documenting an experience like Tristan's, many teachers might be tempted to record his interesting vocabulary (gooey, sticky) and focus only on the language development taking place. Looking deeper, however, teachers could also capitalize on the tactile experiences Tristan was having to "scaffold" new understandings. Because Tristan was able to verbalize his new sensory "findings," his teacher could invite Tristan and the other children nearby to ponder together how the sand became "gooey." There are many science discoveries waiting to happen!

Body Competence

The next story provides a lovely illustration of why sensory interactions with the wonders of nature should be a regular part of children's lives.

"There are children who are very much kinesthetic learners which means they have to touch the thing, hold it, manipulate it, shape it. They have to create these abstractions in their mind through their bodies. I'm finding more and more that if you can engage this type of child through movement you have much less behavior problems because they then have a kind of intrinsic awareness about their own learning style."

Anne Wike
Kinesthetic Specialist
from *Learning With Nature DVD*

Lamb's Ear Landmark
Bode, age 3

I watched as Bode jumped, crawled, and climbed the path, weaving the entire way around the Nature Explore Classroom. He seemed to be in his own world, talking to himself and sometimes stopping to jump in one spot several times. Interestingly, the second time he traveled the path he stopped to touch plants, lingering at the Lamb's Ear and gently cupping it with his hand and then leaning over to rub it on his cheek.

Joyce White, Preschool Teacher
Dimensions Early Education Programs, Lincoln, NE

Insights:

This little boy (who his teacher reports has sensory integration challenges), demonstrated his ability to make sense of his space through his senses. For him, the brain-body connection is especially important. He needs this kind of full-body movement to feel his best self and be ready to take in more information. He was respectful of the living plants, confident, and engaged in exploring. According to his teacher, this same child often is often less successful indoors, more likely to stand away from the group, simply watching what others were doing. Outdoors, his teacher saw him increasing his body control and slowing down to learn from the environment. An interesting note, too, is that as the school year progressed, this routine of traveling the pathway, touching and smelling landmark plants, became his "touchstone" for settling into the day.

Body Competence

It's often easy to discount children's physical and tactile needs as being "unimportant academically," but the teachers in the stories below know otherwise.

Digging
Eli, Preschool child

Whenever Eli was outside, he would dig everywhere and anywhere he could, looking for worms and playing in the dirt. He loved it. The first year I had him, we were only in the planning stages of our Nature Explore Classroom and we did not have a digging space yet. He would make big holes and I was concerned about the safety of other students, of their falling into the holes. I knew that there had to be an area in my Nature Explore Classroom to meet the needs of Eli and the other students who loved digging. The second year he came back and he loved the new Digging Space, our area full of dirt made especially for digging and looking for worms!

Michelle Avilla, Preschool Teacher
Kellom Elementary School, Omaha, NE

We Can Dig It
All ages

Our Dirt Digging Area is one of the most popular places for visitors to our outdoor classroom. We have had wonderful responses from teachers, parents, and children. The teachers are excited to have the Nature Explore Classroom, the parents want to build these at home, and the kids do not want to leave.

Christa Weidner, Naturalist
Jefferson Memorial Forest, Fairdale, KY

Insights:

Outdoor classrooms designed with ample spaces that encourage sensory play help children make synaptic connections that support optimal brain development. Providing children with the freedom to dig, for example, allows them to experience the rich smells, textures and temperature variances of soil. This important sensory information will later serve as a link to new vocabulary words and science understandings. Digging also supports full-body muscle engagement, an important component of healthy physical development.

Tasting the Wind
Henry, age 3

As he ran by me in the Nature Explore Classroom, Henry said, "I just had a taste of that wind!" I asked how he got a taste and he answered, "I tasted the wind with my brain. I tasted it blowing out and blowing in." Henry continued running in the Open Area and I am sure he was getting some good tastes!

Kathy Tichota, Preschool Teacher
Dimensions Early Education Programs, Lincoln, NE

Insights:

How easy it would be to read Henry's story and dismiss it as being merely "cute." It is actually a profound example of Henry's awareness of himself as a learner and of his enjoyment of himself as a sensory being. Both of these things are worthy of celebration, and his wise teacher knew to document his thinking. When children begin to develop meta-cognition (awareness of how they learn), this is a very important developmental milestone.

In the story below, more sensory enjoyment was taking place!

Sense of Smell
Preschool children

Currently we have herbs growing throughout our Nature Explore Classroom, including mint, basil, and rosemary. The children help with picking and packaging the herbs in small bags for their families to take home and use in cooking. Children often remember what the herbs are from the scents left on their fingers! What is also neat is that some parents have even brought recipes back to share at school, taking the experience full circle. Our staff rejoiced this past fall at our Thanksgiving Potluck when a parent used basil from our garden in a giant bowl of spaghetti sauce they had made.

Elena Otto, Assistant Director
Kids and Company Childcare at
Lakeshore Learning Materials, Carson, CA

Insights:

The sense of smell really deepened the experience of taking plants home to families. Children had not just learned about the plants from a book or a screen, but from multi-sensory engagement in growing and caring for them (enough to remember the scents on their fingers)! As you might recall from the Language and Literacy chapter, an experience with growing rosemary inspired a child to write the word to label his plant.

Body Competence

Here, an astute teacher documented a seemingly simple experience, knowing its real value to children.

Rolling
Preschool children, ages 3-5

Many children were on the hill of our Nature Classroom. Natalie lay on the grass and began to roll down the hill. The rest paused in what they were doing to watch. Suddenly there were six or seven children rolling down the hill, laughing and yelling. Several rolled very fast and out of control, while William and Gabby rolled slowly and carefully.

Katie Miller, Preschool Teacher
Russell Child Development Center
Creighton University, Omaha, NE

Insights:

Rolling provides proprioceptive stimulation which helps muscles understand the "feel" of movement. From very early when babies are learning to roll over and then to crawl, the kind of stimulation that rolling provides is important. There are not many opportunities for rolling like this indoors.

Children at Gomez Heritage Elementary School in Omaha, NE, also enjoyed rolling down hills.

Body Competence

The stories below come from environmental educators who know the value that Nature Explore Classrooms in public spaces can provide for young families. Sensory engagement is a theme in both narratives.

Hay, Hay, and More Hay
Liam, age 3

As part of our explorations this fall, I added hay bales and corn stalks to our Messy Materials Area. With each new visitor, excitement grew! Parents and children were jumping, hiding, and playing in the hay from the first moment. However, all was heightened when Liam entered the space. Liam, a frequent visitor to Hidden Hollow, noticed immediately the change to his favorite play place. Running to the hay pile, he asked his mother, "Can I jump in it? Really jump in it?" She encouraged him. "Cool!" he said with a calculated two step run and hop into the hay pile. As the morning progressed, Liam helped me add three more bales to make the pile bigger, tossed and watched strands of hay fall from the air, buried himself and challenged his little brother and mother to find him. He also ran at the pile from different angles and created many different jumps. Remarkably, their family spent over three hours exploring, discovering, and engaging their senses in a hay pile. Thankfully, his mom, an educator herself, understood the sheer value of letting Liam lead his learning. Simply put, a bale of hay opened doors of wonder for him by letting him have that time. Liam returned for a multitude of learning opportunities that fall—exploring and enjoying his special pile of hay in so many ways.

Tobey Eugenio, Environmental Education Specialist
Hidden Hollow at Heritage Museums and Gardens, Sandwich, MA

No Stroller Required
All ages

The Nature Explore Classroom at Nisqually National Wildlife Refuge complements both our formal educational programming and the non-formal visitor opportunities. Instead of being pushed around the trails in strollers, or following an adult leader around, children have meaningful and purposeful hands-on experiences with nature. They can use all their senses to experience nature, while building important observational skills that are the foundation of scientific inquiry. Children can touch, smell, and see the natural world, keeping alive a sense of wonder that will bring lifetime benefits. Children gain confidence and experience that will enable them to further explore, be curious about, and want to spend time in the natural world around them.

Sheila McCartan, Visitor Services Manager
Nisqually National Wildlife Refuge, Olympia, WA

Appropriate Risk-Taking Through Active Play

Linda Verlee Williams states in her book, *Teaching for the Two-Sided Mind*: "Since sensory and motor development are aspects of neural processing and of the development of thinking and reasoning skills, young children should be given as many opportunities to move in as many ways as possible. Most children have an inner sense of the types of movement their body/mind needs. Just as they knew to stand and walk, they know to spin and balance. When young children spend hours spinning or standing on their heads or jumping, they are meeting some inner developmental need which we as adults should honor. With our crowded city streets, small apartments, and the seduction of television, many children do not get the variety of movement experiences they need; some specialists believe that this lack of movement contributes to the learning disorders we see in school." (Williams, 1986)

Just as an active lifestyle is beneficial for adults, children need active play to support healthy bodies. Natural outdoor spaces fully provide that kind of play for young children. For older children who are spending significant time at desks, Nature Explore Classrooms allow them to engage in more full-body learning. When children are able to have that brain-body connection, cognitive and physical development can happen at the same time.

In many urban settings, safe places for active outdoor play in nature can be scarce. Whitcomb W. Hayslip, Los Angeles Unified School District Assistant Superintendent for Early Childhood Education was quoted in an article in the L. A. Times, "A lot of our kids are in environments where they don't have a lot of involvement with the outdoors or the opportunity to be around things where they can climb and explore. The outdoor classrooms become like the backyard – and a stimulating backyard." Los Angeles Unified School District has begun building Nature Explore Classrooms in their schools to ensure that children have daily access to this sensory learning.

"All children, whatever their physical abilities and limitations, need the opportunity to literally reach new heights and run wild. They need the stimulus of risk; they need choices in climbing, sliding, swinging, and so on so that they can determine the excitement and challenge they are ready for." (Greenman, 2007)

Notice how, in the story below, the teacher joins with the children in delighting in the sites and sounds of nature.

Leaf Piles
Infant and Toddler children

One breezy day a small group of children became enthralled with leaves. Children and teachers tossed small yellow leaves that had fallen to the ground back up into the air. We relished the tickles of tumbling leaves on our cheeks, crunched them in our fists and beneath our feet, and watched as wind gusts caught leaves and carried them away. Some children even tried tasting them! We did this for almost 30 minutes, which is a long time for this age group.

Denise Topil, Infant Teacher
Dimensions Early Education Programs, Lincoln, NE

Insights:

Much like Lulu's experience told in an earlier story, this leaf play provided more complete sensory involvement than most indoor explorations could. This wise teacher allowed a variety of exploratory behaviors (from leaves landing on cheeks to leaves ending up in mouths)! As she told us, she watched carefully to be sure children were always safe, but she didn't deprive them the opportunity to engage in some appropriate risk-taking that helped them learn. As a side note, teachers and care providers who spend consistent time in nature with children also reap the benefits of increased activity, fresh air and the inner calmness that comes with it.

In the following story, a teacher supports her toddler children as they challenge themselves to try some new and difficult physical experiences.

Wobbly Winter Walking
Toddler children

Our outdoor exploration of snow and tracks helped develop our body awareness skills. Walking indoors is very different from walking on outdoor surfaces such as snow and woodchips, especially for a two-year-old dressed in many layers of clothes. These experiences in the cold encouraged muscle development and introduced new challenges for my toddlers who were learning to navigate their bodies through space. And children directed their own individual experiences. Miley added more challenge for herself by walking backwards so she could see her tracks as she made them in the snow. This made it more difficult for her to maintain her balance, but she persisted. Hank stomped like a bear he had seen in a book we recently read. I was pleased to see not only his kinesthetic experience, but also this link to literacy. As simple as these activities may seem to an adult, they are the moments that are crucial in early education, providing the foundation of learning for the rest of each child's life.

Kristine Luebbe, Toddler Teacher
Dimensions Early Education Programs, Lincoln, NE

Insights:

This insightful teacher documented the body competence and confidence her toddlers experienced by going outdoors in all kinds of weather. She recognized the opportunities for children to increase coordination as they practiced moving their bodies through space on a variety of terrains. How wonderful that Kristine didn't tell Miley to "be careful" and stop walking backwards, but instead supported her in mastering a new physical challenge. Teachers are able to minimize the risk of taking infants and toddlers outdoors in the cold by monitoring how long they stay out, and by being sure they are dressed appropriately.

Body Competence

Obstacle Course
Lauren, Rachel and Charlene, age 4

Three children created an obstacle course with stepping stones (hollow semi-spheres with a hole in the top for storing on a pole). They stacked the stepping stones on sticks to carry them from one area to another, threading the stick through the holes. They moved them around the space, carefully laying out the course, walking, and bending, lifting, carrying and balancing. When they were finished laying out the course, they carefully stepped from stone to stone, tongues out in concentration, arms stretched out from their sides for balance, and using sticks to steady themselves. They repeated the course many times, varying how they moved. Once they tried it on their toes rather than flat footed. Because the children repeated their actions many times, they had multiple opportunities to use motor planning skills to complete purposeful movement, and develop coordination and balance. The repetition of movement helped children develop muscle memory and body competence.

Ani Ivanov, Teacher
Child Educational Center, La Canada, CA

Insights:

Active play and imaginative thinking are often observed together in Nature Explore Classrooms. As children are experimenting with balance, learning about their own centers of gravity, and figuring out how much muscle power is needed to accomplish tasks, a great deal of problem-solving and creative thinking is taking place. In these situations, it is necessary for adults to understand the learning possibilities. Consistently calling children's attention to the risks undermines their confidence and ability to determine for themselves what is safe and what is not. Adults should stay nearby and give children information if a proposed activity really is too dangerous. Whenever possible, though, it's important to allow children to assess risks for themselves so they gain the skills to keep themselves safe.

Body Competence

Children need places to experiment with what their bodies can do, even when they become older, as the story below illustrates.

Leap Frog
Seventh-grade students

In my Advisory class this year I had several of the athletes, the big, big boys. One day I brought them out to our Nature Explore Classroom for homeroom time and I said, "OK. We're just going to chill out here for awhile." Before too long they were playing leap frog on the giant tree cookies that we had salvaged from a tree that came down on our site. All of the seventh-grade boys were playing! It doesn't matter that you're thirteen and six foot one, or if you're four and three feet high, they love this place and their bodies need it.

Debbie Harris, K-8 Science Department Chairperson
St. Francis Episcopal Day School
Houston, TX

Insights:

All human beings need to move in order to learn, so it's important for students of all ages to have that opportunity. In the story above, the open-ended properties of the tree cookies allowed the "big boys" to use imaginative thinking to create their own game of leap frog. They strengthened their creative thinking skills at the same time they challenged themselves physically.

"When the distance between all the rungs on the climbing net or the ladder is exactly the same, the child has no need to concentrate on where he puts his feet. This lesson cannot be carried over into all the knobbles and asymmetrical forms with which one is confronted throughout life." (Gill, 2005)

Even older children enjoy the freedom to run and jump at Arbor Day Farm's Certified Nature Explore Classroom.

The natural properties of outdoor classrooms provide opportunities for children to learn to safely negotiate the "knobbles and asymmetrical forms" one faces in life. This was true in the story below.

Climbing Wall
Manny, preschool child

SPARK (Supporting Parents and Resilient Kids), the only program of its kind in New England, is a medically-therapeutic childcare facility serving children with complex medical needs and behavior challenges related to trauma. Our Nature Explore Classroom has a high stone wall in back that we typically did not let children climb on. When a teacher noticed Manny climbing it, she reminded him of our rule, though he assured her he knew how to climb and wouldn't get hurt. Ironically, just a few days later our teachers participated in a Nature Explore workshop and the trainer commented, "Oh, what a great rock wall. I bet the kids love to climb this!" Our teachers got together during the workshop and decided to rethink that rule.

Barbara Hughes, Program Coordinator
The SPARK Center, a program of Boston Medical Center, Mattapan, MA

Insights:

Helping children assess risks and make decisions about what they are able to do supports them in better understanding their physical abilities. Often in Nature Explore workshops, educators are encouraged to think collaboratively with their fellow teachers about why they have rules in place, and which ones are really necessary for safety. Some rules are obviously needed to help children avoid hazardous conditions. However, hazards (real dangers such as broken or sharp metal) are different than risks, which can often provide appropriate and beneficial challenges for children. In any case, intense and adequate supervision in the Nature Explore Classroom is always crucial for helping ensure children's safety. In the situation above, one strategy Manny's teacher might have used was to ask him to describe his strategies for keeping himself safe as he climbs the wall. This would reinforce Manny's feelings of body competence and remind him to engage in this activity with appropriate carefulness.

Real Work

"The physical and emotional health of an entire generation and the economic health and security of our nation is at stake. Over the past three decades, childhood obesity rates in America have tripled, and today, nearly one in three children in America are overweight or obese." (First Lady Michelle Obama, 2010)

Raking Mulch
Macek, age 22 months

I noticed that lots of woodchips had migrated out of the Messy Materials Area into the Open Area one day when we were outdoors. I began to rake them back into place as the children were all engaged with each other and my co-teacher. Soon Macek noticed what I was doing and came over to help me. I got him a rake too and he practiced holding it with the tines down, pulling it towards him. All pretty complex movements for a young child, but he was determined to do it just like a teacher.

Kathy Marshall, Toddler Teacher
Dimensions Early Education Programs, Lincoln, NE

Insights:
Outdoor classrooms need ongoing maintenance, and children can be involved in it from the very beginning. Encouraging their participation in caring for the space helps them to feel ownership and pride in their Nature Explore Classrooms, as well as in their physical skills. Even in spaces where maintenance is provided by professional crews, teachers have found it valuable to still engage the children in ongoing caretaking activities.

Hauling Mulch
Jabari and Isabelle, age 4 and James, age 5

The children at our center are responsible for the daily maintenance of the Nature Explore Classroom. This includes the watering and weeding of plants and harvesting herbs. Recently a team of three children had the opportunity to add new woodchips to the Messy Materials Area. So with the use of some strong muscles, a bicycle, and some group cooperation they were able to refill the area.

Elena Otto, Assistant Director
Kids and Company Childcare at
Lakeshore Learning Materials, Carson, CA

Insights:
Having children participate in the real work of caring for their outdoor space helps them be physically healthy. Meaningful activities such as hauling mulch contributes to an active lifestyle that serves children better than contrived exercise such as children's aerobics classes.

Body Competence

Installing a Mosaic
Elementary students, Grades 2-5

It took the entire summer for our group to complete a project that included designing and installing a mosaic in the Artist Garden of our Nature Explore Classroom. The first step was purchasing plates that had been donated to a local charity. Next, each child got to help break a plate of choice, then create a design from the new pieces. Finally we installed the mosaic with the help of local artists and a brick-layer.

Ann Watt, Art Specialist
Dimensions Summer Programs, Lincoln, NE

Wheelbarrow Licensing
Elementary special education students

Working together and responsibility are essential components of gardening with students. In the fall, the students in my primary-aged special education class were given a wheelbarrow licensing test that, upon passing, resulted in full "wheelbarrow privileges." The test was comprised of several steps: filling the wheelbarrow with tools, maneuvering through a set of cones, removing the tools at the garden beds, and driving the wheelbarrow without tipping. Cheered on and encouraged by classmates, each and every student passed the licensing test. Now that students are officially licensed, they are able to independently use the wheelbarrow during garden tasks: plant removal, taking supplies to various areas of the garden, mulching, hauling items to the compost bin and, of course, occasionally giving a classmate a free ride.

Mo Stenger, Special Education Teacher
Beard School, Chicago, IL

Insights:

Notice the fun way this teacher facilitated children's capability to do real work and use real tools in appropriate ways. The large muscle movement, strength, and agility needed for wheelbarrow use are not typically supported indoors. By ensuring that all children knew how to successfully use the wheelbarrows as they were intended, this creative teacher not only increased students' feelings of pride, but also the overall safety of the space.

Body Competence

Digging Up a Marimba
Elementary students

With a donation to our program, we were able to do some renovating in our Infant/Toddler Nature Explore Classroom. Our revised plan called for moving a marimba, and since I was working with a group of 2nd-5th grade students, I asked for volunteers to help me. Three boys set to work digging up the marimba in order to make room for a new, larger Art Area. They worked sporadically for a week using the real long-handled tools and were quite proud of getting it dug out all by themselves!

Kris Van Laningham, School-age Teacher
Dimensions Summer Programs, Lincoln, NE

Insights:

Children and adults often view "work" differently. If we are careful not to give negative messages about difficult physical tasks, children are often eager to participate. They then have the opportunity to develop feelings of pride when they are able to successfully complete a challenging project.

Real Work Equals School Pride
All ages

The bleak Brown Street Academy schoolyard was transformed into a vibrant haven for outdoor education with the installation of Wisconsin's first Certified Nature Explore Outdoor Classroom. Grounded in a participatory design process, the project solicited design ideas and acknowledged site-specific curriculum connections for teachers. The resulting outdoor classroom is used by students during the school day, but is open to the community for use in the evenings and on the weekends. Adjacent to the space is Alice's Garden, a two-acre urban agriculture site, which facilitates agricultural awareness and hands-on projects for school age children. Junior Master Gardeners, a hands-on outdoor gardening program that takes place at Alice's Garden, helps students grades Kindergarten through 5th grade at Brown Street Academy learn the art and the science of growing good food while doing all of the work themselves. However, Alice's Garden serves as more than an outdoor learning environment for our students, it now is a source of school pride: Alice's Garden is centrally featured in a recent mural painted on Brown Street Academy's entry hall, bringing history, education, gardening, and community together.

Lianna Bishop, Administrative Assistant
Resilient Cities, Milwaukee, WI
(Resilient Cities was the leading partner in the Brown Street project)

Healthy Eating

"Overwhelmingly a trend I hear when I talk with certified classrooms about their challenges and successes in their first years, is that gardening is a huge success! So many tell me that having a garden has been instrumental in getting families excited and children involved."

Heather Fox, Nature Explore Education Specialist

Healthy eating habits are encouraged when children are involved in the growing process and understand where the food they eat comes from. Simple gardening activities engage children from planting to weeding to harvesting and cooking.

Tomatoes Taste Like Ketchup
Toddler Group

I am so touched by this memory from a day outdoors last summer. The toddlers were picking and eating cherry tomatoes. One of the toddlers looked to me and said, "Ms. Becky these tomatoes taste like ketchup!"

Becky Grabner, Teacher
Early Childhood Center, Omaha, NE

Insights:

This young toddler made an association between a new food and a familiar food. This was a valuable cognitive experience for her that happened at the same time she gained the health benefits of eating fresh tomatoes.

Picky Eater
Elementary special education students

Our experience with the school garden in the outdoor classroom has been an enormously positive one. We have been fortunate to have a "kitchen-garden expert" at our school, a teacher who won an educational grant to visit kitchen gardens in Australia. Each week she plans a gardening and cooking activity for my students. Her expertise has been invaluable. One of my students with autism, an extremely "picky" eater who would never touch fruits or vegetables, began to sample the fresh garden tomatoes, squash, and other produce that he picked in our school garden.

Tonia Liss, Teacher
Beard School, Chicago, IL

Junior Botanists
Kindergarten children

As part of the kindergarten program each year, the children plant seedlings in our classroom greenhouse. In the early spring, the seedlings are transplanted to the outdoor classroom where they are lovingly cared for as the weather becomes warmer. They enjoy picking lettuce leaves, preparing salads and eating the peas, corn on the cob, cucumbers and green beans that they have grown. Once the leaves begin to change, the children get to experience a fall harvest. One might say that most of the children enjoy this time of year most of all. Our junior botanists experience a sense of wonder as they harvest huge carrots, radishes, watermelons, pumpkins and sunflowers. For a large number of children, this is their first experience of seeing a carrot with its leafy top still attached. The children explore the vegetables with all of their senses and learn more about plant life cycles than any book could teach them. It's amazing to see how many gaps in their learning are filled in by their experiences in the "natural world."

Christine Casalini, Primary Teacher
CA Technologies, CA Montessori Children's Center
Islandia, NY

Children at Dimensions Early Education Programs enjoyed harvesting the carrots they planted.

Sharing the Currants
Garret and Annie, age 5

The children and their families all helped in the creation and planting of our rainbow sensory garden. The parents and children alike were drawn to the smells, colors and textures of the goodies that they grew together. Garret and Annie especially liked picking and eating the currants as they ripened.

Laura Stadtfeld, Director
Laurie's Inn, Casper, WY

Body Competence

Our Backyard
All ages

Our Backyard is what we call our Nature Explore Classroom and it now includes areas for exploration of herb, vegetable and ornamental gardens. Staff members encourage children to touch, smell, taste and eat herbs and vegetables from our garden. Many have noted the shock and surprise on parents' faces when they see their children eating peas, beans, lettuce or even radishes picked straight from the vegetable beds. When children pick, wash and cut vegetables themselves, they are much more likely to try (and like) them. Our Backyard is a window into the natural world that won't save the planet, but will hopefully allow children and their caregivers to have positive experiences there. As children and adults spend more time outside, they begin to understand the importance of clean air, fresh produce and undeveloped land. Children who learn outside want to spend more recreation time there as well. Spending more time outdoors not only increases the amount of children's physical movement but also reduces screen time.

Hillary Olson, former Director of Education
Long Island Children's Museum, Garden City, NY

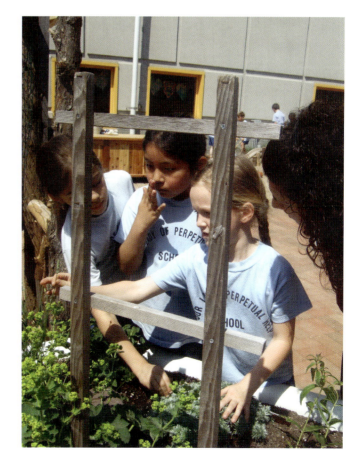

Body Competence

Self-Calming Activities

For overall well-being, children need changes of pace in physical activity throughout their day. Chances to quietly reflect and be calm are just as important as opportunities to be boisterous and active. Nature Explore Classrooms are designed with "hidey spots" (under Weeping Willow trees or nestled between tall grasses) that are just right for one or two children to play quietly together as they learn to self-regulate and enjoy the feelings of calm that nature can inspire.

Children find a "hidey spot" at the Memphis Botanical Garden's Nature Explore Classroom.

A Good Day
All ages

We tell parents if their children come home clean, they didn't have a good day. Parents know this is how it is and this is how they learn. Since we have had our Nature Explore Classroom, behavioral problems have been reduced. Children participate longer in indoor activities and develop problem-solving skills useful both indoors and out. Parents tell us that when they go to kindergarten, they're better prepared.

Ranae Amezquita, Principal
Brooklyn Early Childhood Center
Los Angeles Unified School District, Los Angeles, CA

Growing Calm and Healthy
Preschool child

One afternoon I was playing with a little boy who was bursting with energy when his mom dropped him off in the WEAVE Safehouse Children's School. I could see she was really down and didn't have the energy to play with her son that day. Right away I took him outside to the Messy Materials Area, which has wood chips and log pieces that can be stacked and jumped on. First, the boy stacked the log pieces on each other and said they were pancakes. Luckily before we had to eat the "pancakes," he wanted to play a new game instead. This game was called "hot lava." We spread out the logs and tried to jump from one to another without touching the ground. We both were able to test our agility by trying to jump as far as we could and at the same time stay balanced once we landed on the log. We really worked up a sweat and by the time the boy's mother picked him up he was calm and happy, maybe even ready for a nap!

WEAVE Children's Counselor
WEAVE Safehouse Children's School (at a domestic violence shelter), Sacramento, CA

Insights:

The combination of fun, active play outdoors and positive interaction with a caring adult seemed to turn this child's day around. All children need more opportunities for time in nature, but especially those who are showing signs of restless energy or stress. Wise adults help assess what children need most in order to calm down – a chance to jump from log to log to "let off steam" or a chance to sit quietly under a tree. Fortunately, Nature Explore Classrooms provide both opportunities.

In the story below, innovative educators experimented with nap-time outdoors.

Napping in Nature
Preschool children

Student teachers were skeptical when lab faculty proposed an experiment to move nap time outside when the weather was mild. They later reflected that children were calm, and that even children who did not sleep were relaxed as they listened to the breeze moving through the leaves overhead. For example, one child, Sonora, stated, "When we sleep outside it is better because the wind blows me to sleep." Teachers also reported feeling more relaxed in the outdoor setting. They were less anxious that children who were not sleeping would disturb others.

Jenny Leeper Miller, Master Teacher
Ruth Staples Child Development Laboratory
University of Nebraska, Lincoln, NE

Insights:

Nature provided a lovely soothing element to nap time for these children. Who wouldn't want the wind to blow them to sleep?

As the story below illustrates, sometimes Nature Explore Classrooms support a sense of calm connection with life that can't be found in any other way.

Something for Everyone
Elementary school children

The students in my school are fortunate in many aspects of their lives, however most spend little unstructured time outdoors. Most parents don't feel comfortable letting their children explore in their own backyards, whether it's due to busy schedules or fear of the unknown. So I really want them to have that chance at school. As cliché as it may sound, the more ways I teach, the more types of students I am able to reach, and the outdoor classroom enables my students to learn in many different ways. Surprisingly, many students (even the very active ones) simply enjoy the open green space by stretching their legs and tickling their toes in the green grass while they watch the clouds. There is always something for everyone in our Nature Explore Classroom!

Elizabeth Beckwith, Science Teacher,
St. Martin's Episcopal School, Atlanta, GA

"The symptoms of children with Attention Deficit Disorder (ADD) are relieved after contact with nature. The greener the setting, the more the relief. Children actually perform better on schoolwork after those experiences. By comparison, activities indoors such as watching TV, or outdoors in paved, non-green areas leave children with ADD functioning worse. Maintaining trees and greenery near home and encouraging children with ADD to go out and play may be a compelling approach to helping them cope." (Taylor, Kuo, & Sullivan, 2001)

It's important to note that the Taylor, Kuo and Sullivan quote above makes the point that playing in non-green outdoor areas can often be detrimental for children with ADD. Sending a child to "let off steam" on a noisy, asphalt "playground" will not have the same effect as giving children a chance to be active in a nature-filled outdoor classroom.

"As I watch children play in the outdoor classroom, I witness children's reintroduction to long-term exploratory play, empowering them with a new understanding of cooperation amongst themselves and their peers, and a true satisfaction from the outside world. This reintroduction has proven to improve key concepts in children's basic understanding of the world around them, reflecting positive impacts on their physical and mental health, and their enjoyment of life in general. Outdoor boundaries are now put aside, returning children to a sense of normality in freedom of play."

Catherine Goss, Teacher
Hurlburt Field Air Force Base, Florida

From Dimensions Foundation Research

Excerpts from *Young children develop foundational skills through child-initiated experiences in a Nature Explore Classroom: A single case study in La Canada, California* by Ellen M. Veselack, Lisa Cain-Chang, and Dana L. Miller, 2011.

- The space and nature of the materials in the Nature Explore Classroom provided many opportunities for children to purposefully move and use their bodies (evident in 97% of teachers' observations). Most of the skills children developed centered on whole body experiences as they moved around the NEC. They walked, ran, twirled, crawled, danced, balanced, climbed, jumped, pushed and pedaled tricycles, and used their arms and legs to create momentum on swings. As they exercised their muscles, they developed strength, agility, balance and confidence in their own abilities.

- Children were very active in their play. They frequently carried items from one area to another, filled and pushed the wheelbarrow to carry objects, and built structures with items such as large branches, sticks, rocks, and crates.

- Children...had many opportunities to use fine motor skills and practice eye-hand coordination. They grasped, grabbed, pinched and fingered many objects.

- Children...engaged in tactile experiences that helped them learn about the properties of various materials. For example, they touched cold water and warm sand, and handled prickly sweet gum tree pods, leaves, pine cones, small flowers and rocks. When children discovered moss growing on the side of a tree, they kept coming back to touch it gently. Children went outdoors in the rain and felt raindrops on their heads, hands and bodies and experienced wind on a windy day. These hands-on experiences helped children more fully understand the properties of nature and the objects they were in contact with.

- Children naturally developed kinesthetic skills ...because they had numerous opportunities for whole body movement. The space and layout of the Nature Explore Classroom, because it is well planned and intentional, encouraged children to use their whole bodies in exploration. This is not only impractical indoors but also much less safe than outdoors. The variety and unpredictability of surfaces in the Nature Explore Classroom create opportunities for children to develop greater body competence, because they negotiate the terrain and find secure footing and balance. The Nature Explore Classroom provided the space for children to really move, to use their bodies to the maximum and challenge themselves physically.

- The time spent outdoors afforded children opportunities to repeat kinesthetic experiences over and over, which helped young children build muscle memory, and develop strength and agility. By nature, children are active and the spaciousness of the Nature Explore Classroom allowed them to respond to their bodies' need to move in ways that could not have happened indoors.

Excerpts from *This Never Would Have Happened Indoors: Supporting Preschool-Age Children's Learning in a Nature Explore Classroom in Minnesota* by Vicki Bohling, Cindy Saarela, and Dana L. Miller, 2011.

- Many of these skill development opportunities can be attributed to the unique qualities of outdoor environments that set natural spaces apart from indoor settings. Open spaces allow for voices that can be louder and movement that can be bigger (Frost et al, 2001). A greater range of sensory stimulation occurs outdoors (Olds, 1987) that is different from the predictable walkways, consistent lighting and controlled climates of the indoors. Forgiving ground cover surfaces allow children to take risks, test physical limits, and explore in unique ways.

 To read the complete papers, go to dimensionsfoundation.org/research.

Excerpts taken from *Working Hypotheses* (Insights from Visual Notes-Fall 1999-Spring 2002)

Children who tend to be more kinesthetic seem to more often build structures that are larger scale that they can physically use (this may provide a self-constructed outlet for these children to move).

- When teachers use kinesthetic movement in their teaching, children tend to remember concepts more because their bodies are moving (i.e., kinesthetic movement cements concepts in children's memories). The more experience children have with movement, the more they will be able to remember those movements and think abstractly about them.

"People freely admit they are afraid of accidents in play and want to minimize risk. Yet playgrounds that offer genuine risk tend to have fewer accidents than traditional playgrounds. "Give children real risk and they rise to it; they learn how to handle it. Give them sanitized play spaces, and children often are less conscious of risk and have accidents, or take outlandish risks for the sheer excitement of it all." (Almon, 2009)

Creative Arts

"Creativity is inventing, experimenting, growing, taking risks, breaking rules, making mistakes, and having fun." (This quote is widely attributed to community activist and author, Mary Lou Cook)

Creativity is the way children express their uniqueness. When they act out stories, make music, paint or draw, they make visible what they know, what they feel, and who they are. We've taken the stories people have sent us about children's creative expression in outdoor classrooms and divided them into three categories: Creative Dramatics, Music and Movement, and Visual Art. The Creative Dramatics stories describe the ways children engaged in elaborate, imaginative play that showed what they were thinking about and how they were making sense of their world. The Music and Movement stories reflect the way nature inspired children to create music and then respond to that music through movement. The stories of Visual Art experiences in outdoor classrooms describe children who were truly focused on the process of creation rather than on a product (as is true in developmentally appropriate indoor classrooms as well). In Nature Explore Classrooms, children are frequently seen creating temporary installations with natural materials, and then documenting their three-dimensional work through sketches or photographs.

The stories you're about to read confirm the deep need human beings have to respond to beauty through creative self-expression.

Creative Dramatics

Many adults today express growing concern that children's play is becoming dominated by commercial media. Teachers and parents worry when they see children only acting out familiar television shows or movie characters rather than creating their own ideas. Often times this scripted play appears repetitive and violent. When children have access to open-ended natural materials with which to create their own props, it seems to fuel their innate creativity. The stories in this section depict this kind of rich, inner-fueled dramatic play.

"Here I am king of the forest, there a pirate, now a race car driver, a superhero, a frontier mother, a tiny rabbit. Where can I roam, walk the plank, save the citizenry, keep my baby safe, or find a good carrot? Children like the realism of a stripped down car or boat. But structures that only vaguely represent other things or settings benefit from an ambiguity that allows children's imaginations to take over. The tower that can be a space ship or eagle's nest; the log that's either shark or horse or alligator; the clearing in the bushes or the roofed area that serves as jail, fort, house, or store, all are far superior to expensive castles or rockets or concrete turtles." (Greenman, 2007)

Creative Arts

Creative Arts

Pumpkin Play
Toddler children

I've long known how important it is for infants and toddlers to explore and learn about their environment through their play, but lately I've been realizing how natural materials can inspire such a wide range of creative thinking. A month of exploring pumpkins with toddlers in our Nature Explore Classroom has taught me that a pumpkin can be a "choo choo" or a seat for three. A pumpkin can be a point of negotiation, something heavy to move, or something very exciting to hide!

Heather Fox, Infant Teacher
Dimensions Early Education Programs, Lincoln, NE

Insights:

Toddlers (and older children as well) benefit so much when teachers add seasonal or regional materials to outdoor classrooms in order to spark new kinds of imaginative play. In addition to pumpkins, other good choices might include hay bales, seashells, or even Christmas trees that families are ready to recycle. Caring adults who join in this kind of play with children can model exuberant exploration and a sense of wonder. Engaged caregivers and teachers can also communicate with parents about the value and importance of these kinds of creative dramatics experiences.

Skydiving

Preschool children

"You know what we can play? Let's skydive," Peter whispered to a group of friends on the climbing platform. And just like that, the adventure began! The boys gathered materials (sticks, bark and scraps of cloth) for props such as parachutes and packs. One boy wanted a camera, but the group was unable to decide which material was just the right shape to be a camera. Eager to keep things moving along, Peter told the others, "Pretend it is in the attic and we can't find it. Let's play, dudes!" One by one the boys enjoyed "skydiving" by jumping down from a platform, racing to a far building, tagging it, and racing back.

Sharon Young, Outdoor Classroom Coordinator
Children's Place at St. Andrew's Presbyterian Church
Houston, TX

Insights:

When children use open-ended natural materials to represent familiar items in their creative dramatics play, much complex thinking takes place. Comparisons and choices need to be made, and individual ideas must to be communicated. The boys in the story were communicating their understandings about skydiving (you need a pack with a parachute, and who wouldn't want a photo of themselves doing it?)! They also engaged in social problem-solving and negotiation. Their pretend play was complex and integrated many areas of learning.

Sometimes children need adults to scaffold learning opportunities for them. Skillful teachers recognize when some facilitation needs to occur in order to help children gain the most from an experience. The teachers in the story below were clearly engaged with children in their learning, not merely supervising.

Rainy Day
Preschool children

On a rainy day in February, I was outside with my preschool group. Two girls complained that there was not anything to do in the rain. Rather than list all of the things they could do, I simply picked up a stick and began stirring a puddle. The girls became intrigued and asked what I was doing. "Stirring the soup," I told them. The girls asked if I needed more ingredients and immediately they began collecting nature items such as sweet gum tree pods, grass, and bark and added them to the "soup." For the remainder of our time outside, the girls were in charge of the soup and I was merely one of the cooks.

Kimberly Ryan, Preschool Teacher
Forest Lake Family Center, Forest Lake, MN

Insights:

This teacher seized an opportunity to spark children's imaginations by modeling imaginative play herself.

An important but subtle element in this story is that the children had the opportunity to be "bored." Extended, unstructured times in natural outdoor classrooms require children to think of their own ideas rather than waiting to be entertained or directed by adults.

Willow Pole Horses
Preschool children

"If anyone wants to ride horses, come saddle up!" said Bella. I decided to play along and go for a ride. I pulled a long willow pole out of the rack in the Messy Materials Area. "What color horse would you like to ride?" I asked Landyn, trying to bring him into the activity. He replied, "A Black Beauty!" Gianna told the group she did not want one with a prickly tail. Eventually six children joined in and straddled their poles. A few whinnying sounds could be heard as Bella led us around the cement pad inlaid with leaf prints that's in our Gathering Area. The ride continued with children varying their speed but managing to avoid stepping on each other's poles. I wondered if the children partly enjoyed the ride because of the scraping sounds of the poles on the concrete. One child led us all off the cement and up a grassy slope where we pretended a garden bench was a horse tank. Another child encouraged us all to get our horses a drink before galloping off again.

Holly Murdoch, Preschool Teacher
Dimensions Early Education Programs, Lincoln, NE

Insights:

The combination of imagination and playful movement allowed this group of children to experience whole-body active play of their own creation. The strategy of storing willow poles in a rack in the Messy Materials Area meant that these interesting open-ended materials were readily available to many children. (These materials were not made available until all children in the group had demonstrated the ability to use them safely.) The horse-riding play was both hands-on and minds-on as children decided where their horses would go and what they would do. This teacher also told us that she shared the story with Bella's mother, who reported that Bella had been a little nervous about beginning riding lessons. The teacher and parent agreed that playing horses probably was her way of working through that anxiety.

Creative Arts

The garden at Pioneers Park's Certified Nature Explore Classroom was planted in the shape of a butterfly.

It's Only a Stick
Preschool children

Sticks are deceptively simple. No matter if children are three, four, five, or six years old, each one can find a new adventure in a stick. Outside in our Nature Explore Classroom, we've seen our children use their imaginations to "turn" sticks into magic wands for princess parties, drumsticks to tap a tune on logs, flags to use when pretending to play school, or stick horses to ride on. Sticks are nature's most versatile free learning toys.

Diane Wendelin, Preschool Teacher
Pioneers Park Nature Center, Lincoln, NE

Insights:

In the previous four stories, sticks and branches were featured materials. A free simple toy such as a stick can provide hours of joyful, creative learning experiences. How sad that well-meaning adults sometimes refuse to allow children to play with sticks. With careful supervision and support, adults can help children learn to use these kinds of natural materials safely.

Creative Arts

As Daniel Pink says in his book, *A Whole New Mind*, adults today are preparing children for future jobs we can't even imagine. The skills our children will most likely need include the ability to know what questions to ask, and to see the possibilities in new situations. Play with open-ended materials fully supports this type of learning and thinking. (Pink, 2006)

In the story below, an innovative teacher supports children's science understandings through creative dramatics.

Acting Like Insects
Preschool children

We went on a bug hunt in our outdoor classroom, using a suggestion from a Nature Explore Families' Club activity. We placed a white cloth under a bush and gently shook the branches. It was so exciting to see what fell onto the cloth: ants, spiders, beetles, moths and ladybugs! We looked more closely with our magnifying glasses. We read poems inspired by insects, then we decided to try acting like the insects. As children engaged in this creative dramatics experience, they were strengthening their understandings and their appreciation for the insects.

Cindy Heinzman, Preschool Teacher
Dimensions Early Education Programs, Lincoln, NE

Insights:
Because this teacher gave her students the opportunity to act like insects while they were seeing the real thing, learning could happen rapidly. The "cognitive load" was lessened since children didn't have to both try to imagine what an insect might like while also trying to figure out how the insect might move.

While there is great value in creative dramatics experiences based in reality, there is equally as much value in experiences based in fantasy, such as the one described below.

Fairy Houses
Preschool children

Our Nature Explore Classroom offers a perfect arena for a child's creative development. We have a very special area for building Fairy Houses. The "Fairy Garden" (as we call it) encourages creativity and motor development. The children's gross motor skills are enhanced as they tote around large boards, rocks, tree cookies and stumps to build their structures. Smaller objects such as shells, sticks, and feathers are scattered on the ground, so there is an opportunity for small motor development as well. Children create elaborate, constantly changing playscapes for their pretend fairies. Crayons, paper and various art supplies are also provided so the children can sketch their creations.

Christine Cassalini, Teacher
CA Technologies
CA Montessori Children's Center, Islandia, NY

Insights:
The carefully chosen loose parts and the imaginative arrangement of the environment in this story provided powerful drivers for children's creative play. With no pre-made props, children did their own thinking to invent everything they needed. And, they had the delightful opportunity to visit a world of fantasy for a while.

Read below about how a group of children at a church preschool showed their teachers what they had learned.

How Do You Know They Are Learning?
Preschool children

After listening to their teacher tell a Bible story, a group of preschoolers decided to go to the Music and Movement Area in our Nature Explore Classroom. As they pulled out pieces of cloth to line the music stage, they began assigning roles so they could act out the story. We heard them say things like, "Rosemary gets to be big Jesus first and then we are gonna be the "ciples" (disciples). We gotta sing, cause all the peoples sang to big Jesus! Remember?" As their dramatic play continued, their teacher began to write down their spoken language, take photos of the actual play, and ask questions to determine what they had learned so far about the story. Through this dramatic play sequence, the teacher was able to gather many pieces of documentation for the children's individual portfolios. As she collected these pieces of evidence of their learning, she was able to determine individual levels of social and language development. Through the language of their play, these preschoolers gave us all a little window into their learning!

Pam Scranton, Director
Northminster Learning Center, Peoria, IL

Insights:

The open-ended natural spaces in their outdoor classroom provided these children a way to communicate their learning through creative dramatics. This gave their teacher a valuable opportunity to authentically assess and document what children had understood and internalized about the story they had just heard.

In the next story, a group of elementary school children act on their memories of a book read earlier in the week.

The Tree and the Teacher
Elementary school children

Ivy, Neko, and Rory climbed a tree in our outdoor classroom. I heard them giggling, thinking I had not noticed where they were. They began calling down to me. I stood under the tree, pretending not to know they were up there, or where the voices were coming from. "I didn't know trees could talk," I said, "How do you know my name?" Ivy said," I give oxygen, so don't cut me down!" "Listen to me when I say I have pine stuff in me," added Neko. Then Rory (I am sure recalling the book we read earlier in the week by Shel Silverstein, *The Giving Tree*) said, "Don't be scared of me. Climb me. Use me for a school desk. Come sit under me. Some of my branches are weak so be careful." I thanked the tree and told it I would sit and rest in its shade for a while.

Joyce White, School-age Teacher
Dimensions Summer Programs, Lincoln, NE

Insights:

These children had internalized a story with an environmental message of the importance of trees in our lives. By joining in children's creative play, their teacher was able to assess what the students had learned from the story. Creative dramatics play is an important tool children use to process information and emotions.

Creative Arts

Elementary students visiting Arbor Day Farm's Nature Explore Classroom enjoyed putting on a performance that included creative dramatics, dancing and musical accompaniment.

The story below also involves children who acted out a story. This time it was a prepared play the children performed for an audience. Many teachers report that performing plays in Nature Explore Classrooms seems to keep the experience from becoming too stressful for students or teachers. This is one reason Nature Explore Classrooms typically have an Open Area next to their stage to facilitate these kinds of performances.

Chirps on Stage
Third grade class

My students weren't "cheep-ish" about celebrating community and culture last May. Third graders entertained the school with a performance of *"Pedrito el Pollito Perdido/Pedrito the Lost Little Chick,"* a Cinco de Mayo play based on a new children's book by Oscar Rios Pohrieth, the coordinator for Hispanic services at Lincoln Public Schools, and Dominique Garay, a local poet. The play was a premiere performance on the new stage in our Nature Explore Classroom, a natural learning environment created with community grants and donations from the school's Parent Teacher Organization. Students accompanied their play with handmade musical instruments and Mexican dances. Shows were performed for school audiences during the day and an evening performance entertained parents. The event was part of a year-long celebration of multiculturalism at our school.

Laura Keller, Music Teacher
Sheridan Elementary School, Lincoln, NE

Insights:

Nature Explore Classrooms can provide an ideal place for bringing school communities together through performances such as the one above. Even though this story is included in the Creative Dramatics section, it also provides an example of a meaningful music and movement experience (and a wonderful multicultural exploration). This integrated learning is the richest kind.

Music and Movement

"Movement ties in both hemispheres, allowing people almost their only opportunity to apply both sides of the brain to an effort and attempt to pass information between the right and left hemispheres. For this reason many young children (and older kinesthetic learners) must move to learn." (Languis, Sanders & Tipps, 1980)

The stories below provide examples of how nature, music and movement work so well together. The Body Competence chapter included examples of children's general movement experiences in Nature Explore Classrooms; the movement stories in this chapter primarily depict purposeful movement that is tied to music.

How Does Your Garden Grow?
Toddler children

Our group began exploring seeds; feeling the textures, sorting, breaking apart. Then we planted the seeds in soil, watered them, and waited to see how they would grow. Throughout the process we read books and sang songs that related to plants. One day in the Nature Explore Classroom, as we were checking our garden patch for sprouts, I decided to incorporate some purposeful movement with singing to help children really understand what they were seeing happening. Children curled up into balls pretending to be seeds, wiggled their fingers pretending to be water, then sprouted up and grew tall. Since there were sprouts and plants of varying heights in our garden, I encouraged children to try to imitate the varying sizes and shapes with their bodies.

Kristine Luebbe, Toddler Teacher
Dimensions Early Education Programs, Lincoln, NE

Insights:

Purposeful movement "cements" ideas in children's bodies and minds. In the story above, children listened to words in songs (which related to their seed planting), then acted out the concepts from the songs and from their direct observations. This is a different kind of music and movement experience from one where children listen to wordless music (perhaps created themselves on natural outdoor instruments) and then explore the different ways their bodies are inspired to move. Both are valuable experiences.

Hitting the Note
Preschool child

Nolan began playing the marimba, tapping on it for about three minutes. After that he began humming as he tapped the keys. Next he repeated the process of tapping notes, but this time singing also. He then called out the notes according to the letters on the keys, "A, A, B, E, D, E." Finally he played the keys and sang "ahhh" to each note, trying to get his voice in tune with the note. "I am trying to find a new song. But it does not sound right, does it?" he asked.

Andromahi Harrison, Lead Preschool Teacher
St. Ambrose University Children's Campus
Davenport, IA

Insights:

Nolan was keenly using his sense of hearing and developing a valuable musical understanding as he tried to match notes with his voice. This kind of experimentation with pitch would be difficult to provide in most indoor classrooms. Natural outdoor settings absorb and soften sounds, making them ideal places for musical exploration.

Creative Arts

Playing Music Together
Preschool child

Kevyn, who exhibits autistic characteristics, usually spends his time outside by himself, not interacting with other children or teachers, despite their efforts to include him. One day, Kevyn's class was playing in the Nature Explore Classroom. As usual, Kevyn began outdoor time by walking around by himself. He stopped when he noticed another child, Bobby, at the akambira in the Music Area. Bobby was playing with the small rubber mallets. After watching awhile, Kevyn moved to stand close. A teacher asked Bobby if Kevyn could use one of the mallets and he handed it to her. When she passed it to Kevyn, he began playing also. This was the first time his teacher had seen Kevyn initiating play with another child or even using the same material or toy simultaneously. The two children played together a few minutes before Kevyn moved on. Kevyn has returned to the akambira several times since to make his own music with other children.

Barbara Hughes, Program Coordinator
The SPARK Center, a program of Boston Medical Center, Mattapan, MA

Insights:

Many special education teachers and therapists report the value children with special needs derive from spending time in natural outdoor classrooms. Not only is the calm natural setting conducive to calmer behavior, the interesting materials (such as the natural wood instrument in the story above) seem to inspire children to want to initiate activities or interact with others in ways they usually do not indoors.

Creative Arts

In the story below, nature's beauty inspired some equally beautiful creative expression.

Beautiful Day
Bailey, age 5

While playing in our Nature Explore Classroom, Bailey began spontaneously singing a song. I quickly wrote down her beautiful, heartfelt lyrics:

What a beautiful day

With the sun raising high in the sky.

'Cause the beautiful days mean everything to me.

What a beautiful day, and sing a beautiful day,

Dancing fairies, dancing fairies.

What a beautiful day with sparkling rivers.

The rivers connect to the sea.

Mmm, Mmm

Joyce White, Preschool Teacher
Dimensions Early Education Programs, Lincoln, NE

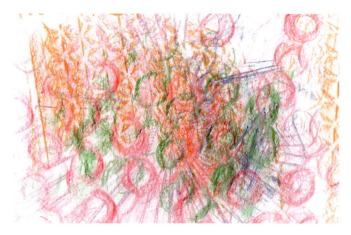

Insights:

Bailey was so inspired by the natural world around her that she created her own song. By writing down the song's words, Bailey's teacher honored and celebrated this authentic self-expression through music.

The story below also provides another example of the calming effects of nature-inspired music.

Healing Through Music
Elementary school student

One of the children I worked with last year liked to have our therapy sessions in the Nature Explore Classroom, sometimes walking on logs or digging in the garden while we talked. As part of therapy she had written a poem describing how her world changed after the sudden death of a close relative. I feel a valuable part of the healing process is to allow children to give voice to their stories. This girl became distressed whenever she tried to read the poem she wrote out loud. I asked her what made her feel the best in the outdoor classroom and she said playing the akambira. We came up with the idea of her playing the akambira until she felt calm, then trying to read the poem, and then playing the akambira again whenever she felt distressed. We tried it and it worked. At first she was able to read about half the poem, and then the entire thing! And whenever she was playing the akambira, she always had a calm smile on her face.

Related by a Counselor and contributed by Beth Hassett, Director of Development and Community Relations, WEAVE Safehouse Children's School (at a domestic violence shelter), Sacramento, CA

Insights:

This is a powerful story of nature's healing power. This perceptive counselor used the girl's enjoyment of the outdoor classroom, and specifically her pleasure in playing the akambira, to help her cope with the death of a loved one. This is a profound experience that will likely be remembered for a lifetime.

Creative Arts

In addition to the value children derive from music and movement experiences outdoors, there is also value for families. Read the story below to see how DKH Academy used their Nature Explore Classroom to build a sense of community.

Family Sing-along
All ages

We decided to invite parents to come to our Nature Explore Classroom for an overnite campout. Of course, a campout wouldn't be complete without roasting marshmallow to make s'mores. Under close supervision, each child roasted a marshmallow to perfection, whether golden brown or burned to a crisp. We sang campfire songs and laughed because we couldn't remember the words. Parents vowed to go home and teach their children classic songs such as "Bingo," "She'll Be Coming Around the Mountain" and "This Land is Your Land." The evening ended with a loud game of flashlight tag, a couple skinned knees and some tired children. Everyone retreated to their tents where the heartwarming lull of family conversation lasted for at least an hour. A couple families abandoned their tents that night for the warmth and coziness of their own bed because the nighttime critter noises were a little scary for their youngsters. But, they came back first thing in the morning to join the group for a pancake and bacon breakfast, break down the tents and start sharing about a wonderful memory that had just been made. Our Nature Explore Outdoor Classroom has been such an enriching addition to our school. It has brought children closer to nature and families closer to each other.

Shelley Easler, Teacher
DKH Academy, Highland Village, TX

Insights:

This is another heartwarming example of how music and nature can bring people together. It's interesting to note that parents remembered the joy in singing traditional songs together and decided they didn't want children to miss out on that kind of shared multi-generational experience.

Children and families at Children's Country Day School in Minnesota also enjoy making music together.

As Bruce Perry says in his book, *Born For Love*, the patterned rhythmic qualities of singing and drumming soothe internal anxiety, promote a sense of camaraderie and community, and reach restorative parts of the brain. This is one reason music is integral to so many cultural celebrations.

Visual Arts

"Art, to me, is the interpretation of the impression which nature makes upon the eye and brain."
(This quote is widely attributed to impressionist artist Childe Hassam.)

Learning to interpret the world around us so that we can find our place in it, and be able to contribute to it, is what education is all about. The process of creating art is one way children can synthesize all that they are learning about the world, especially the natural world. Visual art can be a means of communicating understanding that isn't reliant on spoken language.

In the stories below, educators are comprehensively infusing art into children's learning with nature, even at the earliest ages.

Goldsworthy's Leaves on Rocks
Infant Group

Our infants were encouraged to work together to cover a large stone with freshly fallen leaves from the Discovery Play Garden. This was a project inspired by artist Andy Goldsworthy's work with natural materials. This type of exploration not only provides a unique tactile experience, but also encourages both large and fine motor development and control over wrists, hands and finger movement.

Caitlin Bouse
Atelierista and Nature Curriculum Specialist
Elmhurst Academy of Early Learning, Elmhurst, IL

Insights:

Infants are not often considered artists, but of course they are. This wise educator provides experiences for her youngest students that fuse art with nature and inspires self-expression.

Art Concepts for Infants
Infant Group

Our infants are exposed to art concepts every day in a very natural way. We help them look closely at the colors, shapes, and textures of the items around them. We search for colors in nature like green grass and leaves, white clover, blue flowers and fuzzy purple plants.

Abbie Whisler, Infant Teacher
Dimensions Early Education Programs, Lincoln, NE

Insights:

Intentionally slowing down and providing infants with sensory experiences outdoors honors the way they learn. The information they soak in inspires respect for the natural world and supports creativity. Many visual artists find nature's complexity to be the ideal inspiration for their work.

Creative Arts

The following story illustrates how a change in their outdoor environment inspired children to create richer and more meaningful visual art.

Outside the Box
Preschool children

It was time for a change. The playground wasn't working. The children were fighting over the swings. The older ones wouldn't allow the younger ones on the climber, and groups of children would hide in the plastic playhouses and only come out when it was time to go back inside. Outside play had basically become a war zone, with fights, arguing and tears. But, one day we noticed that something extraordinary was happening. Two children had taken the small plastic shovels and were digging outside the sandbox. They had found a worm and were fascinated. They were not just digging outside the box, they were thinking outside of it too.

We decided that maybe it was time for teachers to do the same. So, we decided to change the playground. All the plastic playthings were removed and the children watched with panicked looks upon their faces. In came giant logs, and large stones, and gardens. As the play yard began to bloom, so did the play of the children. It was soon evident that this is what the children needed. With nature to play with and explore, the children were attentive to their world. As they grew in new ways, we saw those developmental changes reflected in their artwork. We witnessed children who used to quickly scribble their way through art projects actually initiate ones of their own – and with astonishing outcomes! Hanging on the walls of the school now are butterflies with highly detailed mirrored wings and stick bugs with all their legs and antenna cleverly camouflaged in a tree, all inspired by close observations in nature.

Not only did the children's drawing skills seem to improve, but their creativity was enhanced as well. The children collected Maple tree seedpods and used them for insect wings. Cottonwood seeds were used to depict clouds and bunnies in the children's work. Pine cones and attractively colored pebbles were collected and patterns were laid out throughout the play yard, weaving around flowerbeds and down the whimsical river's edge. There seemed to be no end to the possibilities they could discover. None of the children asked about the swings, climber or plastic houses. They were too busy discovering the wonders of nature.

Valerie McCord, Art Teacher
Growing Minds Learning Center, Berkey, OH

Watercolors in the Snow

Jackie and Lily, age 4
Hannah and Asia, age 5

Toward the end of February four girls chose brushes and watercolor paints from a basket in the Nature Art Area and ran over to a large, clear patch of snow. "You have to get it wet – here, watch," said Jackie to Lily. Jackie stroked the brush across the snow, then across the watercolors. She did this several times. A yellow streak appeared in the snow. Hannah said, "Hey, it's working." Lily did the same thing with her brush. "Look at all that wetness," said Jackie. "It's snow water," said Asia. "Yeah, snow water," echoed Jackie. "I'm making a fun picture," said Hannah as she painted with red, back and forth across the snow. "I want black," said Jackie. "Me, too," said Lily. "Me, three," said Hannah (laughing). "I want red now," said Jackie.

Marianne Matlon, Preschool Teacher
Forest Lake Family Center, Forest Lake, MN

Insights:

Because art materials were readily available all year in their Nature Explore Classroom, the girls were able to use a new medium (snow) as part of their art explorations. As they experimented together, they learned about value (the intensity of color), and they learned about their own creativity.

From Dimensions Foundation Research

Excerpts from *Young children develop foundational skills through child-initiated experiences in a Nature Explore Classroom: A single case study in La Canada, California* by Ellen M. Veselack, Lisa Cain-Chang, and Dana L. Miller, 2011.

- We noted that children used critical thinking/problem-solving skills in 56% of the Nature Notes we analyzed. They encountered obstacles as they worked and most often sought answers not from teachers but through experimentation, exploration and testing.

- Teachers trusted children to make decisions and to act on their theories, and allowed them to use materials in unconventional ways, recognizing the learning that was possible for children as they exercised their imaginations and made visual analogies.

Excerpts from *This never would have happened indoors: Supporting preschool-age children's learning in a Nature Explore classroom in Minnesota* by Vicki Bohling, Cindy Saarela, and Dana L. Miller, 2011.

- Young children are instinctually drawn to learning that is concrete, experiential and touched by whimsy. The role of materials cannot be underestimated when creating an environment to support and encourage creative, authentic learning. The basic, un-prescribed qualities of natural items such as sticks and dirt require children to make "something of nothing." The limits to learning are restricted only by the depth of the child's own imagination and resourcefulness. This is the very essence of the critical thinking skills which are highly valued yet elusive in education today.

- Play activity fell into two broad categories: Dramatic/creative scenarios (e.g., playing "pirates" with tree cookies as maps, creating a "cabin" with whole-cut trees) and task-specific themes (e.g., filling pails with dirt, dragging trees, going on a shape hunt.) It was interesting to note that in a number of cases play scenarios reflected local culture ("hunting house", "cabin", "knocked down forest", "muskies") – an indication that children are developing an important "sense of place" (Lester & Maudsley, 2007) as they participate in outdoor activities.

Excerpts from a Focus Group Interview with parents at Forest Lake Family Center by D. Miller, K. Tichota, and V. Bohling, April, 2010.

- It helps children get more creative with what they do. It's continuous play. For example, they're picking up blocks and building a fort – then they're making a fire and roasting marshmallows – then they're playing pirates. Their little minds just run.

 To read the complete papers, go to dimensionsfoundation.org/research.

Visual/Spatial

"Though the centrality of visual/spatial intelligence has long been recognized by researchers who work with adult subjects, relatively little has been definitively established about the development of this set of capacities in children." (Gardner, 1983)

Visual/Spatial Thinking Defined

Visual/spatial thinking is the ability to perceive the visual information in the environment, to represent it internally, to integrate it with other senses and experiences, to derive meaning and understanding, and to perform manipulations and transformations on those perceptions. It is the first language of the brain.

The Benefits of Visual/Spatial Learning

People with highly developed visual/spatial skills pay more attention to the world around them. They notice and appreciate the details of life: the architecture of the buildings in their towns, the kinds of trees in their neighborhoods, the ugly litter that mars the countryside. Visual/spatial skills give people the ability to negotiate well in space: to follow maps, move easily through a forest trail, or maneuver a car into a tight parking space. People need highly developed visual/spatial skills to work in fields such as architecture, engineering, mathematics, geology, sculpture, computer science, aviation, forestry or cartography, but all people, regardless of profession, benefit from strengthening their visual/spatial thinking.

In a world where a confusing array of visual information from television, video games, and advertisements of all types continually bombard our senses, people with highly developed visual/spatial skills are able to make sense of the chaos by "sorting out" the distracting images and focusing on the beauty in nature or pleasing architectural detail. Those who haven't learned to do so often stop paying attention to the details in the world around them as a way to guard against visual overload.

The stories throughout this chapter illustrate ways that meaningful visual/spatial learning is being supported in outdoor classrooms. You'll see how this learning begins with very young children, and continues as those little ones grow into fluent visual/spatial thinkers.

In the following stories, toddlers and preschoolers from the same program enjoy early visual/spatial experiences with natural materials.

Willow Huts
Toddler children

In our toddler outdoor classroom we wanted to make a small space just big enough for one or two children. We wove willow branches into a small hut below an apple tree. When we first built it the teachers were afraid the children would take it apart, but quite the opposite has happened. Toddlers have woven many more sticks and flower stems into the structure. Often it seems to be used as a nest with children pretending to fly in and out.

Ramps and Pathways
Preschool children

In the outdoor classroom our preschool children are able to use "natural loose parts" to explore connections and concepts such as physics, fulcrums, bridges, balance and others. When allowed to manipulate boards, sticks, and wooden tree cookies, children can bridge ideas and hypothesize to discover answers. One day children gleefully discovered they could move water from one place to another safely across a mud hole.

Johanna Booth Miner, Director
Live and Learn Early Learning Center, Lee, NH

Insights:

It's hard for children to develop visual/spatial understandings without the chance to manipulate and transform objects. Nature's "loose parts" provide the ideal objects to explore in this way. This is just one more example of the holistic learning that can happen so well in nature-based outdoor classrooms.

Read the two stories below to see how preschoolers enjoyed some ingenious visual/spatial thinking.

Two Boys and Two Holes
Two boys, age 3

Summer visits to Hidden Hollow's Nature Explore Classroom bring a collection of all age groups. Often our youngest friends find their way to the water pump or sandbox, while our older friends love sitting under the long-legged Rhododendrons to build forts and string up hammocks. On one particular afternoon, two of our youngest friends found their way to the Hidden Hollow Hide-Out. This is a cleared-out underbrush area in a grove of "Rhodies" that is usually occupied with 6 to 8-year-olds. This day it was the focus of two 3-year-old boys. With a clear plan in mind, the boys walked from space to space gathering binoculars, shovels, and watering cans filled with as much water as they could carry. As their parents and I watched, the boys proceeded to work diligently with their shovels—digging, watering, checking their progress with their investigation tools, and then starting the process again. The boys worked on their task for nearly an hour. The finished result was two holes about 3 feet by 3 feet, and 4 inches deep. The observing adults were perplexed by the design until both boys proceeded to squat down, place their backsides into the holes, lean back and lounge against the sides of the holes. The boys had created two side-by-side dirt chairs. The fun didn't end there. The boys next put their feet up and continued to lounge and chat for another 15 minutes in their specially made natural furniture.

Tobey Eugenio, Environmental Education Specialist
Hidden Hollow at Heritage Museums and Gardens
Sandwich, MA

Cedar Maze
Preschool children

An interesting story to come out of our Nature Explore Outdoor Classroom was the creation of a cedar maze. We had some cedar posts from a split-rail fence and wanted to incorporate them into our space. Because we are NAEYC accredited and very close to two major universities, we often have practicum students at our school. This is a great community connection and wonderful way to encourage future educators to respect nature as an important and integral part of any curriculum. Last semester we had a student teacher from the University of North Texas who was very interested in our Nature Explore Classroom. Her semester project was to organize natural materials to be rotated into the different areas, so she decided to design and build a cedar maze from the unused cedar posts. The children love it. We now change the maze every week and encourage our older students to design their own.

Shelley Easler, Teacher
DKH Academy
Highland Village, TX

Insights:

The ability to make natural structures that are large enough to go inside is something unique to nature-based outdoor spaces. This simply does not happen indoors or on traditional playgrounds that do not have these "loose parts" available.

Visual/Spatial

The story below describes a fun and effective way to introduce an outdoor classroom to children when they first begin to use it.

Introducing the Nature Explore Classroom
Preschool children

Each year when I have a new group of children, I find it very important to explore the space together before we start using it. When we first come into our outdoor classroom in the fall, we walk all the pathways before children make their plans so they can discover each area, especially the Garden. This helps them know where they can go, what some of their choices for activities might be, and it sparks their curiosity. Each morning for the first several weeks, we follow the pathways as a group so children can practice with their bodies and begin to feel the entire outdoor classroom. This visual/spatial activity helps children make sense of the space. Throughout the year the pathways became an interesting point of discovery learning as they change with rain, snow, and ice. Sometimes children discover that there are places on the pathways to avoid for safety's sake. Children really get good at gauging the risks they feel comfortable taking. We talk about this together. Many children regularly report to each other when they think a path should be "closed" because it is too slippery. I am happy to have them in charge of not only their learning, but in many ways the use of their own space.

Laurie Flynn, Preschool Teacher
Dimensions Early Education Programs, Lincoln, NE

Insights:

When teachers use visual/spatial strategies (such as walking the pathways of an outdoor classroom with their class, or encouraging children to draw maps of the entire space) deep understandings of how to use the space can develop. The children in this story not only learned to understand their outdoor classroom, but they developed a strong sense of ownership as well.

This next story is about a group of five-year-olds who decided all on their own to go on a "shape hunt" one March day.

Shape Hunt
David, Hannah, Anthony, Foster, all age 5

Hey, it's sunny," said Andrew. "Look, those dead flowers (pointing to sunflower plants near the sidewalk) are circle shapes," said David. "The bricks are rectangles and so is the door!" exclaimed Andrew. "The fence has diamond shapes," said Foster. Hannah looked up into nearby trees. She picked up a forked stick and announced, "A triangle shape." David was over by the teepee structure dragging a recycled Christmas tree. He laid it down parallel to other trees. "A rectangle shape," he said, and traced the outline of it with his finger. Anthony said, "Look, (pointing to an oak tree trunk). See, a line that goes down."

Marianne Matlon, Preschool Teacher
Forest Lake Family Center, Forest Lake, MN

Insights:

If Marianne had not been observing closely, she would have missed the opportunity to understand what rich visual/spatial thinking was happening in such an intrinsically motivating way.

Making a Pond
Thea, age 3

I watched as Thea carefully lined up mini-bricks on the newly installed tree cookie flooring in our Building Area. She created two joining circles and a line of bricks curving away. "This is the pond I went fishing in." Then pointing to the line she continued, "This is the way to get there." I made a sketch of the pond and Thea and I put it in her portfolio. When I showed Thea's mother the sketch, she told me that their family had just been fishing together for the first time the previous weekend and Thea caught the only fish.

Christine Kiewra, Education Specialist
Dimensions Early Education Programs, Lincoln, NE

Insights:

Often when children are able to make three-dimensional models to represent recent experiences, they are able to more fully communicate their thoughts and feelings to others.

"Our findings suggest that visual/spatial fluency is a language and may be the dominant mode of communication for some children. Just as we support reading, writing, and verbal literacy, it is equally important to support visual/spatial development for all children." (Miller, 2004)

Butterfly Pathway
Logan and Monica, age 4

Outside I watched as Logan pointed out a Monarch butterfly that he saw. We had recently read a book about insects and I noted that he recognized the type. When Monica noticed Logan's discovery she ran to the Music and Movement Area, tied scarves to her arms and pretended to be a butterfly. With Logan's help she followed the butterflies' path as they flitted from plant to plant all over the Nature Explore Classroom.

Tami Britton, Preschool Teacher
Dimensions Early Education Programs, Lincoln, NE

Insights:

As these two children practiced visual/spatial thinking, they were also strengthening close observation skills, links to literacy, cooperation and communication, and body competence. This child-led activity showed that Monica and Logan were really "putting it all together!"

Visual/Spatial

Donated Willow
Preschool children

A small army of three-to-five-year-olds greeted a man from our Natural Resources District when he arrived to unload willow branches for our outdoor classroom. Children were eager to help carry the branches, even some that were 20-feet long. They compared the branches to the heights of things they passed, such as trees, the school building, and the climbing structure. Several children used the long branches to see how high they could reach, while others instantly transformed them into fishing poles. Through some creative problem-solving (and with the addition of tree house fabric and clips) children were able to construct a small fort, complete with seating. As they worked, the children discussed angles, balance and size.

Amanda Kelly, Preschool Teacher
Dimensions Early Education Programs, Lincoln, NE

Insights:

The addition of a new material (willow poles), donated by a community supporter (the local Natural Resources District), provided many new opportunities for increased visual/spatial learning. It's important to realize that teachers first assessed children's ability to safely use the willow poles before they were introduced into the outdoor classroom.

"When children actually physically manipulate objects it affects a different part of the brain than just looking at the objects or drawing the objects. It's the whole kinesthetic, tactile manipulation that is making connections in the brain that you can't make with words or in any other way."

Dr. Marjorie Padula, Neuropsychologist
Learning with Nature DVD

Tea Party

Marleigh, Emersyn, and Madison, age 4

Three girls were using all their muscles to move heavy stumps in the Messy Materials Area so they could be closer together. I watched as they scurried to several other areas gathering plant parts from the Garden, scarves from the Music Area, and tree blocks from the Building Area. With lots of discussion about the materials they needed for a "really good" tea party, decisions were made. The scarves became table cloths, the tree cookies the plates, and "snacks and drinks" were made from tree blocks.

Barbie Jensen, Preschool Teacher
Dimensions Early Education Programs, Lincoln, NE

Insights:

The girls used a number of visual/spatial skills to create their tea party. First, they searched their visual memory banks to find visual images of what table cloths, plates, and snacks looked like. Then they searched for the appropriate material that "matched" each visual image. Not only did the open-ended natural materials provide a way for the girls to strengthen visual/spatial thinking, they also inspired Marleigh, Emersyn and Madison to use creative representation and social skills as well.

Read the story below to see how a deceptively simple activity provided valuable visual/spatial experiences.

Discoveries in the Sun and Snow

Preschool children

A light dusting of snow covered the Nature Explore Classroom and the children were eager to discover it in different ways. Logan noticed that snow had covered the steps leading down to the lower level. He offered to help, saying, "This can be my job to clean it up!" As Logan began shoveling, he called to his friends to come and help. Shovels, rakes, sticks and even hands became tools to get the job done. Leighton experimented with making lines in the snow with his rake, and Poppy discovered that with a stick in each hand she could make two lines. As paths were drawn, another child, Henry, noticed his shadow following him. He discovered to his delight that if he stepped forward, his shadow was the same height as mine. When he stepped backward it was even taller! Several children joined in making their shadows move in funny ways, and they were delighted with the shadow shapes they could create with their bodies and tools combined.

Donalyn Katt, Preschool Teacher
Dimensions Early Education Programs, Lincoln, NE

Insights:

This perceptive teacher realized that even a simple activity like shoveling snow could provide a wealth of opportunities for strengthening visual/spatial learning.

A home-school connection is present in the story below.

The Grand Canyon
Kindergarten children

One week, a child in my group had just returned from a vacation to the Grand Canyon. He brought stories, photos, and postcards to share his experiences with his friends. The group was inspired to create the Grand Canyon in the Sand Area by scooping channels and filling them with water. There was lots of discussion about the size of the canyon in relation to the river bed, estimations of how much water the channel would hold, and what the length would be from "rim to rim."

Kris Van Laningham, School-age Teacher
Dimensions Summer Program, Lincoln, NE

Insights:

Thoughtfully designed outdoor classrooms provide great opportunities to capitalize on children's immediate enthusiasms and interests. Because there was a large enough Sand Area to accommodate a whole group of children, this "Grand Canyon" experiment was a rewarding learning experience for children. (And, because the sand box had been designed in a large "L" shape, more children could work without being "on top of" each other.)

Read the story below to find out how another thoughtful design element sparked children's learning.

Bird Blind
Children ages 3 to 10

Our Bird Blind, built in response to requests from first- and second-graders, allows the children to focus on close-up details of birds and bunnies in nature without disturbing them. By observing animals in their natural habitat, the children get to see nature from a different perspective. The bird blind helps students develop observation skills in a fun way. When the children first discovered the bird blind, they looked out of the holes from the front, from the back, and from each shape. They were positioning themselves to see nature through different-shaped "lenses."

Laura Bordow, Lower School Director
Maharishi School, Fairfield, IA

Insights:

By providing a bird blind, teachers made sure that children's interests were validated while their visual/spatial thinking was supported. Looking at the world from multiple perspectives helps children develop stronger visual/spatial skills.

In the following story, a mother was able to look at her son from a whole new perspective.

A Whole New Way to Communicate
Chad, age 6

A few days after her visit to the Nature Explore Classroom with her three children a mother came up to me and told the following story. The mother related how the oldest of her three children had autism. His condition was severe enough that it was often challenging to find things that she could do with all her children together. She had heard about the Nature Explore Classroom and decided one afternoon to take her children there. She had expected her son would only tolerate being there for maybe twenty minutes, but twenty minutes soon turned into an hour… then one hour turned into two. She said her son was totally engaged in the space. His siblings saw him in a whole new light. Most amazing, she said, was that when they got home the son, who seldom communicated with words, excitedly told his dad about his adventures in the outdoor classroom. Then the mother began to cry. She commented that, for many people, exploring and playing in the Nature Explore Classroom was a fun way to spend an afternoon. For her family, it became a whole new way to communicate with their son.

Susie Wirth, Nature Explore Outreach Director, Arbor Day Farm, Nebraska City, NE

Insights:

Children with autism often seem to be strong visual/spatial learners. Teachers, parents and siblings who are able to "hear" what children are saying through their visual/spatial work can learn about what children know and are interested in.

Snake Mazes
Children, ages 6-12

The most talked-about adventure of the summer was the search for a garter snake. The snake was found with only three weeks left of camp, but not a day went by where the children did not try to find him again and again. On the days where our little friend could not be found, the students built wooden mazes under the trees where he was last seen slithering. The children hoped that these structures would help guide the snake back out from under the trees. He was successfully seen two more times that summer.

Tami Clarke, Administrative Coordinator
CA Technologies, CA Academy, Islandia, NY

Insights:

It's important for educators to observe closely when children are interacting with animals and insects in the outdoor classroom. These teachers knew that garter snakes are harmless. There are times, though, when potentially dangerous insects or animals should be taken out of outdoor classrooms. Wasp nests or beehives, for example, should always be removed. Mostly, however, people and critters can co-exist together quite nicely when children are taught to be observers instead of touchers.

Visual/Spatial

In the story below, an older student demonstrated some sophisticated visual/spatial thinking.

My Map
Henry, age 10

After I noticed Henry spending much focused time creating a map of our outdoor classroom, I asked him to describe his work to the rest of the class. "I walked the paths discovering bugs, worms, flowers, and more. I used them as landmarks to make my map," he told us. His map was quite elaborate, and he had obviously looked closely in order to draw with such detail. He also proudly announced to the group (as he was showing his map) that they should be sure to note it was done using a bird's-eye view perspective.

Hannah Wike, School-age Teacher
Dimensions Summer Program, Lincoln NE

Insights:

Students with years of experiences in Nature Explore Classrooms are able to take visual/spatial learning to deeper and deeper levels. Henry's ability to draw from a bird's eye view perspective will help him with future work in higher-level subject areas such as geometry.

Right in Front of Me
All ages

One day as I walked through our Nature Explore Classroom checking supplies and putting things back in the right place, I wondered if the kids who use our space had enough information about what to do when they were out there. For example, did they understand how to use the building materials? Then it struck me that the answer was right in front of me. Every time I go out there, things are different. The blocks and natural materials are in different formations and on different surfaces (like on the building table, the floor, or the picnic table). It was then I realized that they get it, without someone telling them what to do. They just do as they see fit. One day I noticed all the buckets were gone from the Messy Materials Area. I finally found them in the sailboat we have in our Climbing Area. I guess someone must have been in a sinking ship, and all his friends came with buckets to help him bail.

The next day I watched as a brother and sister about four- and six-years-old moved all the building materials in a wheel barrow to a spot next to some bushes. At first I was going to tell them to please leave the materials in the Building Area. Then I heard them saying to each other, "Do you think this is big enough for his whole family?" I asked them what they were doing. They said, "We saw a bunny running under the bushes and thought we would help him by making a home for him and his family." Their Mom smiled and said they had been busy for quite awhile; this was the longest she had seen them work together and not argue in ages. She then said she would have them put it all back when they were done. I invited her to let them leave their project. It was a great house for a rabbit. I told her I would take care of it when they were gone. The children both beamed with pride at their hard work, and continued on. I left the project there for a few days. I never had to go "clean it up." The next time I went out, it was all back on the deck in the Building Area. I think this time it was a skyscraper.

We are having a great time with our Nature Explore Classroom, and the staff is learning each day by watching the children.

Allison Grief, Educational Programs Coordinator
Cornell Cooperative Extension, Suffolk County Farm
& Education Center, Yaphank, NY

Insights:

Wise educators know that nature is a great teacher for children and children are great teachers for adults (if we pay attention). The beauty of natural outdoor classrooms, filled with a bounty of nature's gifts, is that all children are able to use the space "as they see fit." This is what intrinsic motivation is all about, and it's the foundation for effective whole-child learning.

From Dimensions Foundation Research

Excerpts from *Young children develop foundational skills through child-initiated experiences in a Nature Explore Classroom: A single case study in La Canada, California* by Ellen M. Veselack, Lisa Cain-Chang, and Dana L. Miller, 2011.

- We identified children's use of visual/spatial skills in 61% of our Nature Notes. For example, children used visual mapping skills as they created an obstacle course with stepping-stones and then walked the course over and over.

- Children developed visual/spatial skills when they built with blocks and, through practice, gained an understanding of where to place blocks without toppling them. They had to visualize in their minds how to rotate the blocks to stand them up on end and to see where to place them to create the structure they wanted.

- The Nature Explore Classroom provided multiple opportunities for children to develop construction and engineering skills as they engaged in a variety of building experiences (evident in almost half of the Nature Notes – 49%). Some of the specific skills we identified in the data analysis included: learning the concept of sturdy base through experimentation; creating enclosures, walls, tunnels, and bridges; emptying and filling, balancing and bracing objects as they experimented with weight and stability, and basic skills such as propping, piling, and stacking.

Excerpts from *Young Children Learn Through Authentic Play in a Nature Explore Classroom: A White Paper Based on Research Conducted at Dimensions Early Education Programs in Lincoln, NE* by Dana Miller, Kathy Tichota, and Joyce White, 2009

- The organic shapes of natural materials fuel children's creativity and critical thinking, and the non-standard shapes encourage children to make visual analogies (i.e., X "looks like" Y) which is an important visual/spatial skill.

- Open-ended materials allowed children to use their hands and bodies as tools. Every example in this paper of children engaged in authentic play in the Nature Explore Classroom illustrates that children become fully immersed in learning through their senses.

 To read the complete papers, go to dimensionsfoundation.org/research.

Final Thoughts

A Personal Reflection

Throughout this book, inspiring stories illustrate how teachers are working diligently to reconnect children with nature on a daily basis. It's no doubt that the role of the educator or caring adult is crucial to this task, but we might all ask ourselves this question: "When was the last time I reconnected to the natural world to rekindle my own sense of wonder?" Recently, a staff of sixty participants from Prescott Elementary School in Lincoln, Nebraska, visited Arbor Day Farm in Nebraska City, Nebraska to participate in a Nature Explore Workshop titled, "The Wonders of Nature." This experience encourages participants to carve a piece out of their busy lives, slow down, and discover firsthand the beauty and wonder of the natural world. As three trainers and I eagerly awaited the arrival of the group, we were impressed that not only would the entire staff be attending, but also ten parents who had been very successful in their efforts to raise enough money to create a Nature Explore Classroom for their school's community. The school's principal, Ruth Ann Wylie, stood up at the workshop with tears in her eyes and said the creation of the outdoor classroom was a "dream of a lifetime." She discussed how important it was for staff members and parents to have their own

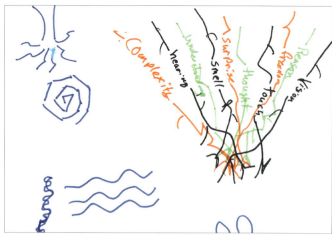

personal experiences connecting with nature, making them better advocates for the benefits of learning with nature. One participant shared a graphic representation that illustrated his personal experience exploring the physical, intellectual and emotional levels of awareness while engaged in the workshop. Outdoor classrooms can serve as rich, nurturing environments that will help foster these areas of awareness in our students as well. Rachel Carson said it best when she wrote, "Those who contemplate the beauty of the earth find reserves of strength that will endure as long as life lasts."

Julie Rose, Nature Explore Educational Services Director, Dimensions Educational Research Foundation, Lincoln, NE

Building for the Future

Today's children are tomorrow's farmers, teachers, musicians, scientists, herpetologists, and engineers. Memorable experiences with nature will help build their skills as well as their appreciation for nature.

Tami Clarke, Administrative Coordinator
CA Technologies, CA Academy, Islandia, NY

All Children Need Nature

The following is an excerpt from the *Universal Principles for Connecting Children With Nature*, written by the World Forum Foundation's Nature Action Collaborative for Children Leadership Team.

We believe it is important that children:

- Have daily access to nature-based outdoor and indoor environments in their early childhood programs and schools.

- Be respected as competent, powerful learners and risk-takers who have a voice in what they create and learn through nature.

- Be supported in developing life skills through holistic nature-based learning.

Read more at worldforumfoundation.org/nature.

References

Almon, J. (2009). The fear of play. *Exchange Magazine,* 31 (2): 42-44

Carson, R. (1965). *The sense of wonder.* New York: Harper & Row

Copley, J.V. (2010). *The young child and mathematics, 2nd edition.* Reston, VA: National Association for the Education of Young Children

Cuppens, V., Rosenow, N., & Wike, J. (2009). *Learning with nature idea book: Creating nurturing outdoor spaces for children.* Lincoln, NE: Arbor Day Foundation

DeVries, R., Reese-Learned, H., & Morgan, P. (1991). Sociomoral development in direct-instruction, eclectic, and constructivist kindergartens: A study of children's enacted interpersonal understanding. *Early Childhood Research Quarterly,* 6 (4): 473-517

Easton, V. (2003). Creative care: Feeling the healing through fingers in the soil. *Pacific Northwest: The Seattle Times Magazine,* November 16, 2003

Edwards, C., Gandini, L. & Forman, G. (1998). *The hundred languages of children: The Reggio Emilia approach – advanced reflections.* Westport, CT: Ablex Publishing

Elkind, D. (2001). *The hurried child.* Cambridge, MA: De Capo Press

Epstein, A. S. (2009). *Me, you, us: Social-emotional learning in preschool.* Ypsilanti, MI: High Scope Press

Furth, H. G. & Wachs, H. (1975). *Thinking goes to school: Piaget's theory in practice.* New York: Oxford University Press

Fjortoft, I. (2001). The natural environment as a playground for children: The impact of outdoor play activities in pre-primary school children. *Early Childhood Education Journal,* 29 (2): 111-117

Galinsky, E. (2010). *Mind in the making: The seven essential life skills every child needs.* New York: Harper Collins Publishers

Gardner, H. (1983) *Frames of mind: The theory of multiple intelligences.* Cambridge, MA: Project Zero Publications of Harvard Press

Gill, T. (2005) *Let our children roam free.* Accessed 2005 at theecologist.org/investigations/society/268765/letourchildrenroamfree

Greenman, J. (1998). *Places for childhoods: Making quality happen in the real world.* Redmond, WA: Exchange Press

Greenman, J. (2007) *Caring spaces, learning places: Children's environments that work.* Redmond, WA: Exchange Press

Helm, J.H. & Katz, L. (2011). *Young investigators: The project approach in the early years.* New York: Teachers College Press

Hensley, D. M. (2006). Discovering science in nature. Accessed April, 2006 at *Early Childhood Today,* scholastic.com

Huh S. & Gordon C.M. (2008). Vitamin D deficiency in children and adolescents: Epidemiology, impact and treatment. *Reviews in Endocrine and Metabolic Disorders,* June 9 (2): 161-70

Kellert, S. (2005). *Building for life: Designing and understanding the human-nature connection.* Washington, DC: Island Press

Languis, M. Sanders, T. & Tipps, S. (1980). *The brain and learning: Directions in early childhood education.* Washington, DC: National Association for the Education of Young Children

Levine, P. & Frederick, A. (1997). *Waking the tiger: Healing trauma.* Berkley, CA: North Atlantic Books

Miller, D. (2007). The seeds of learning: Young children develop important skills through their gardening experiences at a midwestern early education program. *Applied Environmental Education and Communication,* 6 (2): 49-66

Miller, D (2004). More than play: Children learn important skills through visual-spatial work. Accessed 2004 at natureexplore.org/research

National Association for the Education of Young Children & National Council of Teachers of Mathematics joint position statement (2002). *Early childhood mathematics: Promoting good beginnings.* Washington, DC: and Reston, VA: NCTM. Accessed 2002 at naeyc.org/positionstatements/mathematics

National Research Council (1996). *National science education standards.* Washington, DC: National Academy Press

Obama, M. (2010). Let's move address. Accessed 2010 at letsmove.gov

Pica, R. (2010). Why motor skills matter. Accessed 2010 at movingandlearning.com

Pink, D. H. (2006). *A whole new mind: Why right–brainers will rule the future.* New York: Riverhead Books

Rivera, C. (2010). These green thumbs sprout early. *The Los Angeles Times,* December 25, 2010

Root, E.M. (1974). *America's steadfast dream.* Appleton, WI: Western Islands

Roszak, T. (2001). *The voice of the earth: An exploration of ecopsychology.* Grand Rapids, MI: Phanes Press

Rosenow, N. (2011). *Learning to love the Earth and each other.* Spotlight on Young Children and Nature. Washington, DC: NAEYC. Originally published in *Young Children,* 63 (1): 10-13

Smith, C.B. (1997). Vocabulary instruction and reading comprehension. *ERIC Digest,* ED412506. Bloomington, IN: ERIC Clearinghouse

Szakavitz, M. & Perry, B.D. (2010). *Born for love: Why empathy is essential – and endangered.* New York: Harper Collins Publishers

Taylor, A.F., Kuo, F.E. & Sullivan, W.C. (2001). Coping with ADD: The surprising connection to green play settings. *Environment & Behavior,* 33 (1): 54-77

Vygotsky, L. (1962). *Thought and language.* Cambridge, MA: MIT Press

Williams, L.V. (1986). *Teaching for the two-sided mind: A guide to right brain/left brain education.* New York: Simon & Schuster

Wilson, E.O. (1992). *The diversity of life.* Cambridge, MA: Belknap Press of Harvard University Press

Wilson, R. A. (2009). The color green: A 'go' for peace education. *Exchange Magazine,* 31 (3): 40-43

Acknowledgements

Editors and Writers
Christine Kiewra, Nature Explore Education Specialist for Dimensions Educational Research Foundation
Tina Reeble, Nature Explore Education Specialist for Dimensions Educational Research Foundation
Nancy Rosenow, Executive Director of Dimensions Foundation/Nature Explore

Production Director
Valerie Cuppens, Nature Explore Creative Director

Reviewers:
Dr. Dana Miller, Research Director, Dimensions Foundation/Nature Explore Research Director, The Leading Edge/Leadership Institute & Thesis/Portfolio Capstone Programs, Master of Arts in Management Program, Doane College, Lincoln, Nebraska Campus

Julie Rose, Nature Explore Educational Services Director

John Rosenow, Chief Executive Officer, Arbor Day Foundation

Susie Wirth, Nature Explore Outreach Director

Staff at the three Nature Explore Research Sites:

    Child Educational Center Caltech/JPL Community, La Canada, California, Elyssa Nelson, Executive Director, Ellen Veselack and Lisa Cain-Chang, Co-site Research Directors; Joyce White, Nature Explore Site Coordinator

    Dimensions Early Education Programs, Lincoln, NE, Michelle Zimmer, Program Director, Holly Murdoch and Denise Topil, Co-site Research Directors

    Forest Lake Family Center, Forest Lake Minnesota, Cindy Saarela, Program Director, Vicki Bohling and Cindy Saarela, Co-site Research Directors; Kathy Tichota, Nature Explore Site Coordinator

Many thanks to all the Certified Nature Explore Classrooms around the country that sent in stories and photos for this book. We admire the work you are doing to make learning with nature an important part of children's lives:

Arbor Day Farm, Nebraska City, NE; Ascension Lutheran Early Childhood Center, Thousand Oaks, CA; Beard School, Chicago, IL; Blue Hill Elementary School, Blue Hill, NE; Brooklyn Early Childhood Center, Los Angeles Unified School District, Los Angeles, CA; CA Technologies, CA Academy, Islandia, NY; CA Technologies, CA Montessori Children's Center, Islandia, NY; Center for Early Education and Care; Chadron State College, Chadron, NE; Child Educational Center, La Canada, CA; Children's Place at St. Andrew's Presbyterian Church, Houston, TX; Cornell Cooperative Extension, Suffolk County Farm & Education Center, Yaphank, NY; Cyesis Learning Together Programs, Sarasota, FL: Dimensions Early Education Programs, Lincoln, NE; DKH Academy, Highland Village, TX; Early Childhood Center, Omaha, NE; Elmhurst Academy of Early Learning, Elmhurst, IL; Fern Hollow Nature Center, Sewickley, PA; Five Towns Early Learning Center, Inwood, NY; Forest Lake Famly Center, Forest Lake, MN; Gomez Heritage Elementary School, Omaha, NE; Growing Minds Learning Center, Berkey, OH; Hidden Hollow at Heritage Museums and Gardens Sandwich, MA; Hurlburt Field Air Force Base, Florida; Hurlburt Field Library, Hurlburt Air Force Base, FL; James R. Russell Child Development Center, Creighton University, Omaha, NE; Jewel's Learning Center Houston, TX; Kellom Elementary School, Omaha, NE; Kids and Company Childcare at Lakeshore Learning Materials, Carson, CA; Live and Learn Early Learning Center, Lee, NH; Long Island Children's Museum, Garden City, NY; Maharishi School, Fairfield, IA; Middle Country Public Library, Centereach, NY; Nisqually National Wildlife Refuge, Olympia, WA; Northminster Learning Center, Peoria, IL; Pioneers Park Nature Center, Lincoln, NE; Quaker Valley Middle School, Sewickley, PA; Resilient Cities, Milwaukee, WI; Ruth Staples Child Development Laboratory, University of Nebraska-Lincoln; Sheridan Elementary School, Lincoln, NE; St. Ambrose University Children's Campus, Davenport, IA; St. Martin's Episcopal School, Atlanta, GA; St. Thomas Early Learning Center, College Station, TX; Sunset View Farm, Lafayette, NJ; The Family Place Child Development Center, Dallas, TX; The SPARK Center, a program of Boston Medical Center, Mattapan, MA; University of Massachusetts Amherst, Amherst, MA; WEAVE Safehouse Children's School, Sacramento, CA; Webster County Early Learning Center, Blue Hill, NE; WestLake Child Development Center, Houston, TX; Westminster Presbyterian Church Preschool, Westlake Village, CA.

As we create new books, we invite you to send us your stories focused on the following topics: Involving families in nature-based learning; Supporting staff who teach with nature; Utilizing volunteers and effectively maintaining nature-based spaces; New ideas for connecting infants and toddlers with nature.

Please send your stories to info@natureexplore.org

For more information on Nature Explore, and to view video clips that further illustrate growing with nature, please visit natureexplore.org.